C-4493   CAREER EXAMINATION SERIES

This is your
PASSBOOK for...

Temporary Assistance Specialist II

Test Preparation Study Guide
Questions & Answers

COPYRIGHT NOTICE

This book is SOLELY intended for, is sold ONLY to, and its use is RESTRICTED to individual, bona fide applicants or candidates who qualify by virtue of having seriously filed applications for appropriate license, certificate, professional and/or promotional advancement, higher school matriculation, scholarship, or other legitimate requirements of education and/or governmental authorities.

This book is NOT intended for use, class instruction, tutoring, training, duplication, copying, reprinting, excerption, or adaptation, etc., by:

1) Other publishers
2) Proprietors and/or Instructors of "Coaching" and/or Preparatory Courses
3) Personnel and/or Training Divisions of commercial, industrial, and governmental organizations
4) Schools, colleges, or universities and/or their departments and staffs, including teachers and other personnel
5) Testing Agencies or Bureaus
6) Study groups which seek by the purchase of a single volume to copy and/or duplicate and/or adapt this material for use by the group as a whole without having purchased individual volumes for each of the members of the group
7) Et al.

Such persons would be in violation of appropriate Federal and State statutes.

PROVISION OF LICENSING AGREEMENTS – Recognized educational, commercial, industrial, and governmental institutions and organizations, and others legitimately engaged in educational pursuits, including training, testing, and measurement activities, may address request for a licensing agreement to the copyright owners, who will determine whether, and under what conditions, including fees and charges, the materials in this book may be used them. In other words, a licensing facility exists for the legitimate use of the material in this book on other than an individual basis. However, it is asseverated and affirmed here that the material in this book CANNOT be used without the receipt of the express permission of such a licensing agreement from the Publishers. Inquiries re licensing should be addressed to the company, attention rights and permissions department.

All rights reserved, including the right of reproduction in whole or in part, in any form or by any means, electronic or mechanical, including photocopying, recording, or by any information storage and retrieval system, without permission in writing from the Publisher.

Copyright © 2025 by
National Learning Corporation

212 Michael Drive, Syosset, NY 11791
(516) 921-8888 • www.passbooks.com
E-mail: info@passbooks.com

PASSBOOK® SERIES

THE *PASSBOOK® SERIES* has been created to prepare applicants and candidates for the ultimate academic battlefield – the examination room.

At some time in our lives, each and every one of us may be required to take an examination – for validation, matriculation, admission, qualification, registration, certification, or licensure.

Based on the assumption that every applicant or candidate has met the basic formal educational standards, has taken the required number of courses, and read the necessary texts, the *PASSBOOK® SERIES* furnishes the one special preparation which may assure passing with confidence, instead of failing with insecurity. Examination questions – together with answers – are furnished as the basic vehicle for study so that the mysteries of the examination and its compounding difficulties may be eliminated or diminished by a sure method.

This book is meant to help you pass your examination provided that you qualify and are serious in your objective.

The entire field is reviewed through the huge store of content information which is succinctly presented through a provocative and challenging approach – the question-and-answer method.

A climate of success is established by furnishing the correct answers at the end of each test.

You soon learn to recognize types of questions, forms of questions, and patterns of questioning. You may even begin to anticipate expected outcomes.

You perceive that many questions are repeated or adapted so that you can gain acute insights, which may enable you to score many sure points.

You learn how to confront new questions, or types of questions, and to attack them confidently and work out the correct answers.

You note objectives and emphases, and recognize pitfalls and dangers, so that you may make positive educational adjustments.

Moreover, you are kept fully informed in relation to new concepts, methods, practices, and directions in the field.

You discover that you are actually taking the examination all the time: you are preparing for the examination by "taking" an examination, not by reading extraneous and/or supererogatory textbooks.

In short, this PASSBOOK®, used directedly, should be an important factor in helping you to pass your test.

TEMPORARY ASSISTANCE SPECIALIST II

DUTIES
As a Temporary Assistance Specialist II, you would under general direction, supervise Temporary Assistance Specialists I or other subordinate staff in the maintenance, development, dissemination and evaluation of supportive programs or systems designed to increase the economic security of low-income working families and assist low-income work capable individuals in entering or re-entering the workforce. You also may monitor and provide technical assistance to local social services districts regarding federal and State program requirements and policies; coordinate interagency efforts; develop linkages with other local organizations; oversee assigned local district administration of programs; assist State and local officials in meeting program requirements or measures of efficiency and effectiveness; develop draft policies and procedures related to new and revised temporary and transitional programs; participate in training local districts and subordinate staff in program requirements; supervise staff; or directly administer benefit programs.

SCOPE OF THE EXAMINATION
The written test will cover knowledge, skills and/or abilities in such areas as:

1. Administrative techniques and practices;
2. Ensuring effective inter/intra-agency communications;
3. Supervision;
4. Evaluating conclusions based on factual information; and
5. Preparing written material.

HOW TO TAKE A TEST

I. YOU MUST PASS AN EXAMINATION

A. *WHAT EVERY CANDIDATE SHOULD KNOW*

Examination applicants often ask us for help in preparing for the written test. What can I study in advance? What kinds of questions will be asked? How will the test be given? How will the papers be graded?

As an applicant for a civil service examination, you may be wondering about some of these things. Our purpose here is to suggest effective methods of advance study and to describe civil service examinations.

Your chances for success on this examination can be increased if you know how to prepare. Those "pre-examination jitters" can be reduced if you know what to expect. You can even experience an adventure in good citizenship if you know why civil service exams are given.

B. *WHY ARE CIVIL SERVICE EXAMINATIONS GIVEN?*

Civil service examinations are important to you in two ways. As a citizen, you want public jobs filled by employees who know how to do their work. As a job seeker, you want a fair chance to compete for that job on an equal footing with other candidates. The best-known means of accomplishing this two-fold goal is the competitive examination.

Exams are widely publicized throughout the nation. They may be administered for jobs in federal, state, city, municipal, town or village governments or agencies.

Any citizen may apply, with some limitations, such as the age or residence of applicants. Your experience and education may be reviewed to see whether you meet the requirements for the particular examination. When these requirements exist, they are reasonable and applied consistently to all applicants. Thus, a competitive examination may cause you some uneasiness now, but it is your privilege and safeguard.

C. *HOW ARE CIVIL SERVICE EXAMS DEVELOPED?*

Examinations are carefully written by trained technicians who are specialists in the field known as "psychological measurement," in consultation with recognized authorities in the field of work that the test will cover. These experts recommend the subject matter areas or skills to be tested; only those knowledges or skills important to your success on the job are included. The most reliable books and source materials available are used as references. Together, the experts and technicians judge the difficulty level of the questions.

Test technicians know how to phrase questions so that the problem is clearly stated. Their ethics do not permit "trick" or "catch" questions. Questions may have been tried out on sample groups, or subjected to statistical analysis, to determine their usefulness.

Written tests are often used in combination with performance tests, ratings of training and experience, and oral interviews. All of these measures combine to form the best-known means of finding the right person for the right job.

II. HOW TO PASS THE WRITTEN TEST

A. NATURE OF THE EXAMINATION

To prepare intelligently for civil service examinations, you should know how they differ from school examinations you have taken. In school you were assigned certain definite pages to read or subjects to cover. The examination questions were quite detailed and usually emphasized memory. Civil service exams, on the other hand, try to discover your present ability to perform the duties of a position, plus your potentiality to learn these duties. In other words, a civil service exam attempts to predict how successful you will be. Questions cover such a broad area that they cannot be as minute and detailed as school exam questions.

In the public service similar kinds of work, or positions, are grouped together in one "class." This process is known as *position-classification*. All the positions in a class are paid according to the salary range for that class. One class title covers all of these positions, and they are all tested by the same examination.

B. FOUR BASIC STEPS

1) Study the announcement

How, then, can you know what subjects to study? Our best answer is: "Learn as much as possible about the class of positions for which you've applied." The exam will test the knowledge, skills and abilities needed to do the work.

Your most valuable source of information about the position you want is the official exam announcement. This announcement lists the training and experience qualifications. Check these standards and apply only if you come reasonably close to meeting them.

The brief description of the position in the examination announcement offers some clues to the subjects which will be tested. Think about the job itself. Review the duties in your mind. Can you perform them, or are there some in which you are rusty? Fill in the blank spots in your preparation.

Many jurisdictions preview the written test in the exam announcement by including a section called "Knowledge and Abilities Required," "Scope of the Examination," or some similar heading. Here you will find out specifically what fields will be tested.

2) Review your own background

Once you learn in general what the position is all about, and what you need to know to do the work, ask yourself which subjects you already know fairly well and which need improvement. You may wonder whether to concentrate on improving your strong areas or on building some background in your fields of weakness. When the announcement has specified "some knowledge" or "considerable knowledge," or has used adjectives like "beginning principles of…" or "advanced … methods," you can get a clue as to the number and difficulty of questions to be asked in any given field. More questions, and hence broader coverage, would be included for those subjects which are more important in the work. Now weigh your strengths and weaknesses against the job requirements and prepare accordingly.

3) Determine the level of the position

Another way to tell how intensively you should prepare is to understand the level of the job for which you are applying. Is it the entering level? In other words, is this the position in which beginners in a field of work are hired? Or is it an intermediate or advanced level? Sometimes this is indicated by such words as "Junior" or "Senior" in the class title. Other jurisdictions use Roman numerals to designate the level – Clerk I, Clerk II, for example. The word "Supervisor" sometimes appears in the title. If the level is not indicated by the title, check the description of duties. Will you be working under very close supervision, or will you have responsibility for independent decisions in this work?

4) Choose appropriate study materials

Now that you know the subjects to be examined and the relative amount of each subject to be covered, you can choose suitable study materials. For beginning level jobs, or even advanced ones, if you have a pronounced weakness in some aspect of your training, read a modern, standard textbook in that field. Be sure it is up to date and has general coverage. Such books are normally available at your library, and the librarian will be glad to help you locate one. For entry-level positions, questions of appropriate difficulty are chosen – neither highly advanced questions, nor those too simple. Such questions require careful thought but not advanced training.

If the position for which you are applying is technical or advanced, you will read more advanced, specialized material. If you are already familiar with the basic principles of your field, elementary textbooks would waste your time. Concentrate on advanced textbooks and technical periodicals. Think through the concepts and review difficult problems in your field.

These are all general sources. You can get more ideas on your own initiative, following these leads. For example, training manuals and publications of the government agency which employs workers in your field can be useful, particularly for technical and professional positions. A letter or visit to the government department involved may result in more specific study suggestions, and certainly will provide you with a more definite idea of the exact nature of the position you are seeking.

III. KINDS OF TESTS

Tests are used for purposes other than measuring knowledge and ability to perform specified duties. For some positions, it is equally important to test ability to make adjustments to new situations or to profit from training. In others, basic mental abilities not dependent on information are essential. Questions which test these things may not appear as pertinent to the duties of the position as those which test for knowledge and information. Yet they are often highly important parts of a fair examination. For very general questions, it is almost impossible to help you direct your study efforts. What we can do is to point out some of the more common of these general abilities needed in public service positions and describe some typical questions.

1) General information

Broad, general information has been found useful for predicting job success in some kinds of work. This is tested in a variety of ways, from vocabulary lists to questions about current events. Basic background in some field of work, such as sociology or economics, may be sampled in a group of questions. Often these are principles which have become familiar to most persons through exposure rather than through formal training. It is difficult to advise you how to study for these questions; being alert to the world around you is our best suggestion.

2) Verbal ability

An example of an ability needed in many positions is verbal or language ability. Verbal ability is, in brief, the ability to use and understand words. Vocabulary and grammar tests are typical measures of this ability. Reading comprehension or paragraph interpretation questions are common in many kinds of civil service tests. You are given a paragraph of written material and asked to find its central meaning.

3) Numerical ability

Number skills can be tested by the familiar arithmetic problem, by checking paired lists of numbers to see which are alike and which are different, or by interpreting charts and graphs. In the latter test, a graph may be printed in the test booklet which you are asked to use as the basis for answering questions.

4) Observation

A popular test for law-enforcement positions is the observation test. A picture is shown to you for several minutes, then taken away. Questions about the picture test your ability to observe both details and larger elements.

5) Following directions

In many positions in the public service, the employee must be able to carry out written instructions dependably and accurately. You may be given a chart with several columns, each column listing a variety of information. The questions require you to carry out directions involving the information given in the chart.

6) Skills and aptitudes

Performance tests effectively measure some manual skills and aptitudes. When the skill is one in which you are trained, such as typing or shorthand, you can practice. These tests are often very much like those given in business school or high school courses. For many of the other skills and aptitudes, however, no short-time preparation can be made. Skills and abilities natural to you or that you have developed throughout your lifetime are being tested.

Many of the general questions just described provide all the data needed to answer the questions and ask you to use your reasoning ability to find the answers. Your best preparation for these tests, as well as for tests of facts and ideas, is to be at your physical and mental best. You, no doubt, have your own methods of getting into an exam-taking mood and keeping "in shape." The next section lists some ideas on this subject.

IV. KINDS OF QUESTIONS

Only rarely is the "essay" question, which you answer in narrative form, used in civil service tests. Civil service tests are usually of the short-answer type. Full instructions for answering these questions will be given to you at the examination. But in case this is your first experience with short-answer questions and separate answer sheets, here is what you need to know:

1) Multiple-choice Questions

Most popular of the short-answer questions is the "multiple choice" or "best answer" question. It can be used, for example, to test for factual knowledge, ability to solve problems or judgment in meeting situations found at work.

A multiple-choice question is normally one of three types—
- It can begin with an incomplete statement followed by several possible endings. You are to find the one ending which *best* completes the statement, although some of the others may not be entirely wrong.
- It can also be a complete statement in the form of a question which is answered by choosing one of the statements listed.

- It can be in the form of a problem – again you select the best answer.

Here is an example of a multiple-choice question with a discussion which should give you some clues as to the method for choosing the right answer:

When an employee has a complaint about his assignment, the action which will *best* help him overcome his difficulty is to
    A. discuss his difficulty with his coworkers
    B. take the problem to the head of the organization
    C. take the problem to the person who gave him the assignment
    D. say nothing to anyone about his complaint

In answering this question, you should study each of the choices to find which is best. Consider choice "A" – Certainly an employee may discuss his complaint with fellow employees, but no change or improvement can result, and the complaint remains unresolved. Choice "B" is a poor choice since the head of the organization probably does not know what assignment you have been given, and taking your problem to him is known as "going over the head" of the supervisor. The supervisor, or person who made the assignment, is the person who can clarify it or correct any injustice. Choice "C" is, therefore, correct. To say nothing, as in choice "D," is unwise. Supervisors have and interest in knowing the problems employees are facing, and the employee is seeking a solution to his problem.

2) True/False Questions

The "true/false" or "right/wrong" form of question is sometimes used. Here a complete statement is given. Your job is to decide whether the statement is right or wrong.

SAMPLE: A roaming cell-phone call to a nearby city costs less than a non-roaming call to a distant city.

This statement is wrong, or false, since roaming calls are more expensive.

This is not a complete list of all possible question forms, although most of the others are variations of these common types. You will always get complete directions for answering questions. Be sure you understand *how* to mark your answers – ask questions until you do.

V. RECORDING YOUR ANSWERS

Computer terminals are used more and more today for many different kinds of exams.
For an examination with very few applicants, you may be told to record your answers in the test booklet itself. Separate answer sheets are much more common. If this separate answer sheet is to be scored by machine – and this is often the case – it is highly important that you mark your answers correctly in order to get credit.
An electronic scoring machine is often used in civil service offices because of the speed with which papers can be scored. Machine-scored answer sheets must be marked with a pencil, which will be given to you. This pencil has a high graphite content which responds to the electronic scoring machine. As a matter of fact, stray dots may register as answers, so do not let your pencil rest on the answer sheet while you are pondering the correct answer. Also, if your pencil lead breaks or is otherwise defective, ask for another.

Since the answer sheet will be dropped in a slot in the scoring machine, be careful not to bend the corners or get the paper crumpled.

The answer sheet normally has five vertical columns of numbers, with 30 numbers to a column. These numbers correspond to the question numbers in your test booklet. After each number, going across the page are four or five pairs of dotted lines. These short dotted lines have small letters or numbers above them. The first two pairs may also have a "T" or "F" above the letters. This indicates that the first two pairs only are to be used if the questions are of the true-false type. If the questions are multiple choice, disregard the "T" and "F" and pay attention only to the small letters or numbers.

Answer your questions in the manner of the sample that follows:

32. The largest city in the United States is
    A. Washington, D.C.
    B. New York City
    C. Chicago
    D. Detroit
    E. San Francisco

1) Choose the answer you think is best. (New York City is the largest, so "B" is correct.)
2) Find the row of dotted lines numbered the same as the question you are answering. (Find row number 32)
3) Find the pair of dotted lines corresponding to the answer. (Find the pair of lines under the mark "B.")
4) Make a solid black mark between the dotted lines.

VI. BEFORE THE TEST

Common sense will help you find procedures to follow to get ready for an examination. Too many of us, however, overlook these sensible measures. Indeed, nervousness and fatigue have been found to be the most serious reasons why applicants fail to do their best on civil service tests. Here is a list of reminders:

- Begin your preparation early – Don't wait until the last minute to go scurrying around for books and materials or to find out what the position is all about.
- Prepare continuously – An hour a night for a week is better than an all-night cram session. This has been definitely established. What is more, a night a week for a month will return better dividends than crowding your study into a shorter period of time.
- Locate the place of the exam – You have been sent a notice telling you when and where to report for the examination. If the location is in a different town or otherwise unfamiliar to you, it would be well to inquire the best route and learn something about the building.
- Relax the night before the test – Allow your mind to rest. Do not study at all that night. Plan some mild recreation or diversion; then go to bed early and get a good night's sleep.
- Get up early enough to make a leisurely trip to the place for the test – This way unforeseen events, traffic snarls, unfamiliar buildings, etc. will not upset you.
- Dress comfortably – A written test is not a fashion show. You will be known by number and not by name, so wear something comfortable.

- Leave excess paraphernalia at home – Shopping bags and odd bundles will get in your way. You need bring only the items mentioned in the official notice you received; usually everything you need is provided. Do not bring reference books to the exam. They will only confuse those last minutes and be taken away from you when in the test room.
- Arrive somewhat ahead of time – If because of transportation schedules you must get there very early, bring a newspaper or magazine to take your mind off yourself while waiting.
- Locate the examination room – When you have found the proper room, you will be directed to the seat or part of the room where you will sit. Sometimes you are given a sheet of instructions to read while you are waiting. Do not fill out any forms until you are told to do so; just read them and be prepared.
- Relax and prepare to listen to the instructions
- If you have any physical problem that may keep you from doing your best, be sure to tell the test administrator. If you are sick or in poor health, you really cannot do your best on the exam. You can come back and take the test some other time.

VII. AT THE TEST

The day of the test is here and you have the test booklet in your hand. The temptation to get going is very strong. Caution! There is more to success than knowing the right answers. You must know how to identify your papers and understand variations in the type of short-answer question used in this particular examination. Follow these suggestions for maximum results from your efforts:

1) Cooperate with the monitor
The test administrator has a duty to create a situation in which you can be as much at ease as possible. He will give instructions, tell you when to begin, check to see that you are marking your answer sheet correctly, and so on. He is not there to guard you, although he will see that your competitors do not take unfair advantage. He wants to help you do your best.

2) Listen to all instructions
Don't jump the gun! Wait until you understand all directions. In most civil service tests you get more time than you need to answer the questions. So don't be in a hurry. Read each word of instructions until you clearly understand the meaning. Study the examples, listen to all announcements and follow directions. Ask questions if you do not understand what to do.

3) Identify your papers
Civil service exams are usually identified by number only. You will be assigned a number; you must not put your name on your test papers. Be sure to copy your number correctly. Since more than one exam may be given, copy your exact examination title.

4) Plan your time
Unless you are told that a test is a "speed" or "rate of work" test, speed itself is usually not important. Time enough to answer all the questions will be provided, but this does not mean that you have all day. An overall time limit has been set. Divide the total time (in minutes) by the number of questions to determine the approximate time you have for each question.

5) Do not linger over difficult questions

If you come across a difficult question, mark it with a paper clip (useful to have along) and come back to it when you have been through the booklet. One caution if you do this – be sure to skip a number on your answer sheet as well. Check often to be sure that you have not lost your place and that you are marking in the row numbered the same as the question you are answering.

6) Read the questions

Be sure you know what the question asks! Many capable people are unsuccessful because they failed to *read* the questions correctly.

7) Answer all questions

Unless you have been instructed that a penalty will be deducted for incorrect answers, it is better to guess than to omit a question.

8) Speed tests

It is often better NOT to guess on speed tests. It has been found that on timed tests people are tempted to spend the last few seconds before time is called in marking answers at random – without even reading them – in the hope of picking up a few extra points. To discourage this practice, the instructions may warn you that your score will be "corrected" for guessing. That is, a penalty will be applied. The incorrect answers will be deducted from the correct ones, or some other penalty formula will be used.

9) Review your answers

If you finish before time is called, go back to the questions you guessed or omitted to give them further thought. Review other answers if you have time.

10) Return your test materials

If you are ready to leave before others have finished or time is called, take ALL your materials to the monitor and leave quietly. Never take any test material with you. The monitor can discover whose papers are not complete, and taking a test booklet may be grounds for disqualification.

VIII. EXAMINATION TECHNIQUES

1) Read the general instructions carefully. These are usually printed on the first page of the exam booklet. As a rule, these instructions refer to the timing of the examination; the fact that you should not start work until the signal and must stop work at a signal, etc. If there are any *special* instructions, such as a choice of questions to be answered, make sure that you note this instruction carefully.

2) When you are ready to start work on the examination, that is as soon as the signal has been given, read the instructions to each question booklet, underline any key words or phrases, such as *least, best, outline, describe* and the like. In this way you will tend to answer as requested rather than discover on reviewing your paper that you *listed without describing*, that you selected the *worst* choice rather than the *best* choice, etc.

3) If the examination is of the objective or multiple-choice type – that is, each question will also give a series of possible answers: A, B, C or D, and you are called upon to select the best answer and write the letter next to that answer on your answer paper – it is advisable to start answering each question in turn. There may be anywhere from 50 to 100 such questions in the three or four hours allotted and you can see how much time would be taken if you read through all the questions before beginning to answer any. Furthermore, if you come across a question or group of questions which you know would be difficult to answer, it would undoubtedly affect your handling of all the other questions.

4) If the examination is of the essay type and contains but a few questions, it is a moot point as to whether you should read all the questions before starting to answer any one. Of course, if you are given a choice – say five out of seven and the like – then it is essential to read all the questions so you can eliminate the two that are most difficult. If, however, you are asked to answer all the questions, there may be danger in trying to answer the easiest one first because you may find that you will spend too much time on it. The best technique is to answer the first question, then proceed to the second, etc.

5) Time your answers. Before the exam begins, write down the time it started, then add the time allowed for the examination and write down the time it must be completed, then divide the time available somewhat as follows:
    - If 3-1/2 hours are allowed, that would be 210 minutes. If you have 80 objective-type questions, that would be an average of 2-1/2 minutes per question. Allow yourself no more than 2 minutes per question, or a total of 160 minutes, which will permit about 50 minutes to review.
    - If for the time allotment of 210 minutes there are 7 essay questions to answer, that would average about 30 minutes a question. Give yourself only 25 minutes per question so that you have about 35 minutes to review.

6) The most important instruction is to *read each question* and make sure you know what is wanted. The second most important instruction is to *time yourself properly* so that you answer every question. The third most important instruction is to *answer every question*. Guess if you have to but include something for each question. Remember that you will receive no credit for a blank and will probably receive some credit if you write something in answer to an essay question. If you guess a letter – say "B" for a multiple-choice question – you may have guessed right. If you leave a blank as an answer to a multiple-choice question, the examiners may respect your feelings but it will not add a point to your score. Some exams may penalize you for wrong answers, so in such cases *only*, you may not want to guess unless you have some basis for your answer.

7) Suggestions
    a. Objective-type questions
        1. Examine the question booklet for proper sequence of pages and questions
        2. Read all instructions carefully
        3. Skip any question which seems too difficult; return to it after all other questions have been answered
        4. Apportion your time properly; do not spend too much time on any single question or group of questions

5. Note and underline key words – *all, most, fewest, least, best, worst, same, opposite,* etc.
6. Pay particular attention to negatives
7. Note unusual option, e.g., unduly long, short, complex, different or similar in content to the body of the question
8. Observe the use of "hedging" words – *probably, may, most likely,* etc.
9. Make sure that your answer is put next to the same number as the question
10. Do not second-guess unless you have good reason to believe the second answer is definitely more correct
11. Cross out original answer if you decide another answer is more accurate; do not erase until you are ready to hand your paper in
12. Answer all questions; guess unless instructed otherwise
13. Leave time for review

   b. Essay questions
   1. Read each question carefully
   2. Determine exactly what is wanted. Underline key words or phrases.
   3. Decide on outline or paragraph answer
   4. Include many different points and elements unless asked to develop any one or two points or elements
   5. Show impartiality by giving pros and cons unless directed to select one side only
   6. Make and write down any assumptions you find necessary to answer the questions
   7. Watch your English, grammar, punctuation and choice of words
   8. Time your answers; don't crowd material

8) Answering the essay question

Most essay questions can be answered by framing the specific response around several key words or ideas. Here are a few such key words or ideas:

M's: manpower, materials, methods, money, management
P's: purpose, program, policy, plan, procedure, practice, problems, pitfalls, personnel, public relations

   a. Six basic steps in handling problems:
   1. Preliminary plan and background development
   2. Collect information, data and facts
   3. Analyze and interpret information, data and facts
   4. Analyze and develop solutions as well as make recommendations
   5. Prepare report and sell recommendations
   6. Install recommendations and follow up effectiveness

   b. Pitfalls to avoid
   1. *Taking things for granted* – A statement of the situation does not necessarily imply that each of the elements is necessarily true; for example, a complaint may be invalid and biased so that all that can be taken for granted is that a complaint has been registered

2. *Considering only one side of a situation* – Wherever possible, indicate several alternatives and then point out the reasons you selected the best one
3. *Failing to indicate follow up* – Whenever your answer indicates action on your part, make certain that you will take proper follow-up action to see how successful your recommendations, procedures or actions turn out to be
4. *Taking too long in answering any single question* – Remember to time your answers properly

IX. AFTER THE TEST

Scoring procedures differ in detail among civil service jurisdictions although the general principles are the same. Whether the papers are hand-scored or graded by machine we have described, they are nearly always graded by number. That is, the person who marks the paper knows only the number – never the name – of the applicant. Not until all the papers have been graded will they be matched with names. If other tests, such as training and experience or oral interview ratings have been given, scores will be combined. Different parts of the examination usually have different weights. For example, the written test might count 60 percent of the final grade, and a rating of training and experience 40 percent. In many jurisdictions, veterans will have a certain number of points added to their grades.

After the final grade has been determined, the names are placed in grade order and an eligible list is established. There are various methods for resolving ties between those who get the same final grade – probably the most common is to place first the name of the person whose application was received first. Job offers are made from the eligible list in the order the names appear on it. You will be notified of your grade and your rank as soon as all these computations have been made. This will be done as rapidly as possible.

People who are found to meet the requirements in the announcement are called "eligibles." Their names are put on a list of eligible candidates. An eligible's chances of getting a job depend on how high he stands on this list and how fast agencies are filling jobs from the list.

When a job is to be filled from a list of eligibles, the agency asks for the names of people on the list of eligibles for that job. When the civil service commission receives this request, it sends to the agency the names of the three people highest on this list. Or, if the job to be filled has specialized requirements, the office sends the agency the names of the top three persons who meet these requirements from the general list.

The appointing officer makes a choice from among the three people whose names were sent to him. If the selected person accepts the appointment, the names of the others are put back on the list to be considered for future openings.

That is the rule in hiring from all kinds of eligible lists, whether they are for typist, carpenter, chemist, or something else. For every vacancy, the appointing officer has his choice of any one of the top three eligibles on the list. This explains why the person whose name is on top of the list sometimes does not get an appointment when some of the persons lower on the list do. If the appointing officer chooses the second or third eligible, the No. 1 eligible does not get a job at once, but stays on the list until he is appointed or the list is terminated.

X. HOW TO PASS THE INTERVIEW TEST

The examination for which you applied requires an oral interview test. You have already taken the written test and you are now being called for the interview test – the final part of the formal examination.

You may think that it is not possible to prepare for an interview test and that there are no procedures to follow during an interview. Our purpose is to point out some things you can do in advance that will help you and some good rules to follow and pitfalls to avoid while you are being interviewed.

What is an interview supposed to test?

The written examination is designed to test the technical knowledge and competence of the candidate; the oral is designed to evaluate intangible qualities, not readily measured otherwise, and to establish a list showing the relative fitness of each candidate – as measured against his competitors – for the position sought. Scoring is not on the basis of "right" and "wrong," but on a sliding scale of values ranging from "not passable" to "outstanding." As a matter of fact, it is possible to achieve a relatively low score without a single "incorrect" answer because of evident weakness in the qualities being measured.

Occasionally, an examination may consist entirely of an oral test – either an individual or a group oral. In such cases, information is sought concerning the technical knowledges and abilities of the candidate, since there has been no written examination for this purpose. More commonly, however, an oral test is used to supplement a written examination.

Who conducts interviews?

The composition of oral boards varies among different jurisdictions. In nearly all, a representative of the personnel department serves as chairman. One of the members of the board may be a representative of the department in which the candidate would work. In some cases, "outside experts" are used, and, frequently, a businessman or some other representative of the general public is asked to serve. Labor and management or other special groups may be represented. The aim is to secure the services of experts in the appropriate field.

However the board is composed, it is a good idea (and not at all improper or unethical) to ascertain in advance of the interview who the members are and what groups they represent. When you are introduced to them, you will have some idea of their backgrounds and interests, and at least you will not stutter and stammer over their names.

What should be done before the interview?

While knowledge about the board members is useful and takes some of the surprise element out of the interview, there is other preparation which is more substantive. It *is* possible to prepare for an oral interview – in several ways:

1) Keep a copy of your application and review it carefully before the interview

This may be the only document before the oral board, and the starting point of the interview. Know what education and experience you have listed there, and the sequence and dates of all of it. Sometimes the board will ask you to review the highlights of your experience for them; you should not have to hem and haw doing it.

2) Study the class specification and the examination announcement

Usually, the oral board has one or both of these to guide them. The qualities, characteristics or knowledges required by the position sought are stated in these documents. They offer valuable clues as to the nature of the oral interview. For example, if the job involves supervisory responsibilities, the announcement will usually indicate that knowledge of modern supervisory methods and the qualifications of the candidate as a supervisor will be tested. If so, you can expect such questions, frequently in the form of a hypothetical situation which you are expected to solve. NEVER go into an oral without knowledge of the duties and responsibilities of the job you seek.

3) Think through each qualification required

Try to visualize the kind of questions you would ask if you were a board member. How well could you answer them? Try especially to appraise your own knowledge and background in each area, *measured against the job sought*, and identify any areas in which you are weak. Be critical and realistic – do not flatter yourself.

4) Do some general reading in areas in which you feel you may be weak

For example, if the job involves supervision and your past experience has NOT, some general reading in supervisory methods and practices, particularly in the field of human relations, might be useful. Do NOT study agency procedures or detailed manuals. The oral board will be testing your understanding and capacity, not your memory.

5) Get a good night's sleep and watch your general health and mental attitude

You will want a clear head at the interview. Take care of a cold or any other minor ailment, and of course, no hangovers.

What should be done on the day of the interview?

Now comes the day of the interview itself. Give yourself plenty of time to get there. Plan to arrive somewhat ahead of the scheduled time, particularly if your appointment is in the fore part of the day. If a previous candidate fails to appear, the board might be ready for you a bit early. By early afternoon an oral board is almost invariably behind schedule if there are many candidates, and you may have to wait. Take along a book or magazine to read, or your application to review, but leave any extraneous material in the waiting room when you go in for your interview. In any event, relax and compose yourself.

The matter of dress is important. The board is forming impressions about you – from your experience, your manners, your attitude, and your appearance. Give your personal appearance careful attention. Dress your best, but not your flashiest. Choose conservative, appropriate clothing, and be sure it is immaculate. This is a business interview, and your appearance should indicate that you regard it as such. Besides, being well groomed and properly dressed will help boost your confidence.

Sooner or later, someone will call your name and escort you into the interview room. *This is it.* From here on you are on your own. It is too late for any more preparation. But remember, you asked for this opportunity to prove your fitness, and you are here because your request was granted.

What happens when you go in?

The usual sequence of events will be as follows: The clerk (who is often the board stenographer) will introduce you to the chairman of the oral board, who will introduce you to the other members of the board. Acknowledge the introductions before you sit down. Do not be surprised if you find a microphone facing you or a stenotypist sitting by. Oral interviews are usually recorded in the event of an appeal or other review.

Usually the chairman of the board will open the interview by reviewing the highlights of your education and work experience from your application – primarily for the benefit of the other members of the board, as well as to get the material into the record. Do not interrupt or comment unless there is an error or significant misinterpretation; if that is the case, do not hesitate. But do not quibble about insignificant matters. Also, he will usually ask you some question about your education, experience or your present job – partly to get you to start talking and to establish the interviewing "rapport." He may start the actual questioning, or turn it over to one of the other members. Frequently, each member undertakes the questioning on a particular area, one in which he is perhaps most competent, so you can expect each member to participate in the examination. Because time is limited, you may also expect some rather abrupt switches in the direction the questioning takes, so do not be upset by it. Normally, a board member will not pursue a single line of questioning unless he discovers a particular strength or weakness.

After each member has participated, the chairman will usually ask whether any member has any further questions, then will ask you if you have anything you wish to add. Unless you are expecting this question, it may floor you. Worse, it may start you off on an extended, extemporaneous speech. The board is not usually seeking more information. The question is principally to offer you a last opportunity to present further qualifications or to indicate that you have nothing to add. So, if you feel that a significant qualification or characteristic has been overlooked, it is proper to point it out in a sentence or so. Do not compliment the board on the thoroughness of their examination – they have been sketchy, and you know it. If you wish, merely say, "No thank you, I have nothing further to add." This is a point where you can "talk yourself out" of a good impression or fail to present an important bit of information. Remember, *you close the interview yourself*.

The chairman will then say, "That is all, Mr. _____, thank you." Do not be startled; the interview is over, and quicker than you think. Thank him, gather your belongings and take your leave. Save your sigh of relief for the other side of the door.

How to put your best foot forward

Throughout this entire process, you may feel that the board individually and collectively is trying to pierce your defenses, seek out your hidden weaknesses and embarrass and confuse you. Actually, this is not true. They are obliged to make an appraisal of your qualifications for the job you are seeking, and they want to see you in your best light. Remember, they must interview all candidates and a non-cooperative candidate may become a failure in spite of their best efforts to bring out his qualifications. Here are 15 suggestions that will help you:

1) Be natural – Keep your attitude confident, not cocky

If you are not confident that you can do the job, do not expect the board to be. Do not apologize for your weaknesses, try to bring out your strong points. The board is interested in a positive, not negative, presentation. Cockiness will antagonize any board member and make him wonder if you are covering up a weakness by a false show of strength.

2) Get comfortable, but don't lounge or sprawl

Sit erectly but not stiffly. A careless posture may lead the board to conclude that you are careless in other things, or at least that you are not impressed by the importance of the occasion. Either conclusion is natural, even if incorrect. Do not fuss with your clothing, a pencil or an ashtray. Your hands may occasionally be useful to emphasize a point; do not let them become a point of distraction.

3) Do not wisecrack or make small talk

This is a serious situation, and your attitude should show that you consider it as such. Further, the time of the board is limited – they do not want to waste it, and neither should you.

4) Do not exaggerate your experience or abilities

In the first place, from information in the application or other interviews and sources, the board may know more about you than you think. Secondly, you probably will not get away with it. An experienced board is rather adept at spotting such a situation, so do not take the chance.

5) If you know a board member, do not make a point of it, yet do not hide it

Certainly you are not fooling him, and probably not the other members of the board. Do not try to take advantage of your acquaintanceship – it will probably do you little good.

6) Do not dominate the interview

Let the board do that. They will give you the clues – do not assume that you have to do all the talking. Realize that the board has a number of questions to ask you, and do not try to take up all the interview time by showing off your extensive knowledge of the answer to the first one.

7) Be attentive

You only have 20 minutes or so, and you should keep your attention at its sharpest throughout. When a member is addressing a problem or question to you, give him your undivided attention. Address your reply principally to him, but do not exclude the other board members.

8) Do not interrupt

A board member may be stating a problem for you to analyze. He will ask you a question when the time comes. Let him state the problem, and wait for the question.

9) Make sure you understand the question

Do not try to answer until you are sure what the question is. If it is not clear, restate it in your own words or ask the board member to clarify it for you. However, do not haggle about minor elements.

10) Reply promptly but not hastily

A common entry on oral board rating sheets is "candidate responded readily," or "candidate hesitated in replies." Respond as promptly and quickly as you can, but do not jump to a hasty, ill-considered answer.

11) Do not be peremptory in your answers

A brief answer is proper – but do not fire your answer back. That is a losing game from your point of view. The board member can probably ask questions much faster than you can answer them.

12) Do not try to create the answer you think the board member wants

He is interested in what kind of mind you have and how it works – not in playing games. Furthermore, he can usually spot this practice and will actually grade you down on it.

13) Do not switch sides in your reply merely to agree with a board member

Frequently, a member will take a contrary position merely to draw you out and to see if you are willing and able to defend your point of view. Do not start a debate, yet do not surrender a good position. If a position is worth taking, it is worth defending.

14) Do not be afraid to admit an error in judgment if you are shown to be wrong
   The board knows that you are forced to reply without any opportunity for careful consideration. Your answer may be demonstrably wrong. If so, admit it and get on with the interview.

15) Do not dwell at length on your present job
   The opening question may relate to your present assignment. Answer the question but do not go into an extended discussion. You are being examined for a *new* job, not your present one. As a matter of fact, try to phrase ALL your answers in terms of the job for which you are being examined.

Basis of Rating
   Probably you will forget most of these "do's" and "don'ts" when you walk into the oral interview room. Even remembering them all will not ensure you a passing grade. Perhaps you did not have the qualifications in the first place. But remembering them will help you to put your best foot forward, without treading on the toes of the board members.
   Rumor and popular opinion to the contrary notwithstanding, an oral board wants you to make the best appearance possible. They know you are under pressure – but they also want to see how you respond to it as a guide to what your reaction would be under the pressures of the job you seek. They will be influenced by the degree of poise you display, the personal traits you show and the manner in which you respond.

ABOUT THIS BOOK

   This book contains tests divided into Examination Sections. Go through each test, answering every question in the margin. We have also attached a sample answer sheet at the back of the book that can be removed and used. At the end of each test look at the answer key and check your answers. On the ones you got wrong, look at the right answer choice and learn. Do not fill in the answers first. Do not memorize the questions and answers, but understand the answer and principles involved. On your test, the questions will likely be different from the samples. Questions are changed and new ones added. If you understand these past questions you should have success with any changes that arise. Tests may consist of several types of questions. We have additional books on each subject should more study be advisable or necessary for you. Finally, the more you study, the better prepared you will be. This book is intended to be the last thing you study before you walk into the examination room. Prior study of relevant texts is also recommended. NLC publishes some of these in our Fundamental Series. Knowledge and good sense are important factors in passing your exam. Good luck also helps. So now study this Passbook, absorb the material contained within and take that knowledge into the examination. Then do your best to pass that exam.

EXAMINATION SECTION

COMMUNICATION

EXAMINATION SECTION
TEST 1

DIRECTIONS: Each question or incomplete statement is followed by several suggested answers or completions. Select the one that BEST answers the question or completes the statement. *PRINT THE LETTER OF THE CORRECT ANSWER IN THE SPACE AT THE RIGHT.*

1. In some agencies the counsel to the agency head is given the right to bypass the chain of command and issue orders directly to the staff concerning matters that involve certain specific processes and practices.
 This situation MOST nearly illustrates the principle of _____ authority.
 A. the acceptance theory of
 B. multiple-linear
 C. splintered
 D. functional

2. It is commonly understood that communication is an important part of the administrative process.
 Which of the following is NOT a valid principle of the communication process in administration?
 A. The channels of communication should be spontaneous.
 B. The lines of communication should be as direct and as short as possible.
 C. Communications should be authenticated.
 D. The persons serving in communications centers should be competent.

3. Of the following, the one factor which is generally considered LEAST essential to successful committee operations is
 A. stating a clear definition of the authority and scope of the committee
 B. selecting the committee chairman carefully
 C. limiting the size of the committee to four persons
 D. limiting the subject matter to that which can be handled in group discussion

4. Of the following, the failure by line managers to accept and appreciate the benefits and limitations of a new program or system VERY FREQUENTLY can be traced to the
 A. budgetary problems involved
 B. resultant need to reduce staff
 C. lack of controls it engenders
 D. failure of top management to support its implementation

5. If a manager were thinking about using a committee of subordinates to solve an operating problem, which of the following would generally NOT be an advantage of such use of the committee approach?
 A. Improved coordination
 B. Low cost
 C. Increased motivation
 D. Integrated judgment

6. Every supervisor has many occasions to lead a conference or participate in a conference of some sort.
Of the following statements that pertain to conferences and conference leadership, which is generally considered to be MOST valid?
   A. Since World War II, the trend has been toward fewer shared decisions and more conferences.
   B. The most important part of a conference leader's job is to direct discussion.
   C. In providing opportunities for group interaction, management should avoid consideration of its past management philosophy.
   D. A good administrator cannot lead a good conference if he is a poor public speaker.

7. Of the following, it is usually LEAST desirable for a conference leader to
   A. call the name of a person after asking a question
   B. summarize proceedings periodically
   C. make a practice of repeating questions
   D. ask a question without indicating who is to reply

8. Assume that, in a certain organization, a situation has developed in which there is little difference in status or authority between individuals.
Which of the following would be the MOST likely result with regard to communication in this organization?
   A. Both the accuracy and flow of communication will be improved.
   B. Both the accuracy and flow of communication will substantially decrease.
   C. Employees will seek more formal lines of communication.
   D. Neither the flow nor the accuracy of communication will be improved over the former hierarchical structure.

9. The main function of many agency administrative officers is "information management." Information that is received by an administrative officer may be classified as active or passive, depending upon whether or not it requires the recipient to take some action.
Of the following, the item received which is clearly the MOST active information is
   A. an appointment of a new staff member
   B. a payment voucher for a new desk
   C. a press release concerning a past event
   D. the minutes of a staff meeting

10. Of the following, the one LEAST considered to be a communication barrier is
   A. group feedback   B. charged words
   C. selective perception   D. symbolic meanings

11. Management studies support the hypothesis that, in spite of the tendency of employees to censor the information communicated to their supervisor, subordinates are more likely to communicate problem-oriented information UPWARD when they have a
    A. long period of service in the organization
    B. high degree of trust in the supervisor
    C. high educational level
    D. low status on the organizational ladder

11.____

12. Electronic data processing equipment can produce more information faster than can be generated by any other means.
In view of this, the MOST important problem faced by management at present is to
    A. keep computers fully occupied
    B. find enough computer personnel
    C. assimilate and properly evaluate the information
    D. obtain funds to establish appropriate information systems

12.____

13. A well-designed management information system essentially provides each executive and manager the information he needs for
    A. determining computer time requirements
    B. planning and measuring results
    C. drawing a new organization chart
    D. developing a new office layout

13.____

14. It is generally agreed that management policies should be periodically reappraised and restated in accordance with current conditions.
Of the following, the approach which would be MOST effective in determining whether a policy should be revised is to
    A. conduct interviews with staff members at all levels in order to ascertain the relationship between the policy and actual practice
    B. make proposed revisions in the policy and apply it to current problems
    C. make up hypothetical situations using both the old policy and a revised version in order to make comparisons
    D. call a meeting of top level staff in order to discuss ways of revising the policy

14.____

15. Your superior has asked you to notify division employees of an important change in one of the operating procedures described in the division manual. Every employee presently has a copy of this manual.
Which of the following is normally the MOST practical way to get the employees to understand such a change?
    A. Notify each employee individually of the change and answer any questions he might have
    B. Send a written notice to key personnel, directing them to inform the people under them

15.____

3

C. Call a general meeting, distribute a corrected page for the manual, and discuss the change
D. Send a memo to employees describing the change in general terms and asking them to make the necessary corrections in their copies of the manual

16. Assume that the work in your department involves the use of any technical terms.
    In such a situation, when you are answering inquiries from the general public, it would usually be BEST to
    A. use simple language and avoid the technical terms
    B. employ the technical terms whenever possible
    C. bandy technical terms freely, but explain each term in parentheses
    D. apologize if you are forced to use a technical term

16.____

17. Suppose that you receive a telephone call from someone identifying himself as an employee in another city department who asks to be given information which your own department regards as confidential.
    Which of the following is the BEST way of handling such a request?
    A. Give the information requested, since your caller as official standing
    B. Grant the request, provided the caller gives you a signed receipt
    C. Refuse the request, because you have no way of knowing whether the caller is really who he claims to be
    D. Explain that the information is confidential and inform the caller of the channels he must go through to have the information released to him

17.____

18. Studies show that office employees place high importance on the social and human aspects of the organization. What office employees like best about their jobs is the kind of people with whom they work. So strive hard to group people who are most likely to get along well together.
    Based on this information, it is MOST reasonable to assume that office workers are most pleased to work in a group which
    A. is congenial   B. has high productivity
    C. allows individual creativity   D. is unlike other groups

18.____

19. A certain supervisor does not compliment members of his staff when they come up with good ideas. He feels that coming up with good ideas is part of the job and does not merit special attention.
    This supervisor's practice is
    A. *poor*, because recognition for good ideas is a good motivator
    B. *poor*, because the staff will suspect that the supervisor has no good ideas of his own
    C. *good*, because it is reasonable to assume that employees will tell their supervisor of ways to improve office practice
    D. *good*, because the other members of the staff are not made to seem inferior by comparison

19.____

20. Some employees of a department have sent an anonymous letter containing many complaints to the department head.
Of the following, what is this MOST likely to show about the department?
   A. It is probably a good place to work.
   B. Communications are probably poor.
   C. The complaints are probably unjustified.
   D. These employees are probably untrustworthy.

21. Which of the following actions would usually be MOST appropriate for a supervisor to take after receiving an instruction sheet from his superior explaining a new procedure which is to be followed?
   A. Put the instruction sheet aside temporarily until he determines what is wrong with the old procedure.
   B. Call his superior and ask whether the procedure is one he must implement immediately.
   C. Write a memorandum to the superior asking for more details.
   D. Try the new procedure and advise the superior of any problems or possible improvements.

22. Of the following, which one is considered the PRIMARY advantage of using a committee to resolved a problem in an organization?
   A. No one person will be held accountable for the decision since a group of people was involved.
   B. People with different backgrounds give attention to the problem.
   C. The decision will take considerable time so there is unlikely to be a decision that will later be regretted.
   D. One person cannot dominate the decision-making process.

23. Employees in a certain office come to their supervisor with all their complaints about the office and the work. Almost every employee has had at least one minor complaint at some time.
The situation with respect to complaints in this office may BEST be described as probably
   A. *good*; employees who complain care about their jobs and work hard
   B. *good*; grievances brought out into the open can be corrected
   C. *bad*; only serious complaints should be discussed
   D. *bad*; it indicates the staff does not have confidence in the administration

24. The administrator who allows his staff to suggest ways to do their work will usually find that
   A. this practice contributes to high productivity
   B. the administrator's ideas produce greater output
   C. clerical employees suggest inefficient work methods
   D. subordinate employees resent performing a management function

25. The MAIN purpose for a supervisor's questioning the employees at a conference he is holding is to
    A. stress those areas of information covered but not understood by the participants
    B. encourage participants to think through the problem under discussion
    C. catch those subordinates who are not paying attention
    D. permit the more knowledgeable participants to display their grasp of the problems being discussed

KEY (CORRECT ANSWERS)

1.	D		11.	B
2.	A		12.	C
3.	C		13.	B
4.	D		14.	A
5.	B		15.	C
6.	B		16.	A
7.	C		17.	D
8.	D		18.	A
9.	A		19.	A
10.	A		20.	B

21.	D
22.	B
23.	B
24.	A
25.	B

TEST 2

DIRECTIONS: Each question or incomplete statement is followed by several suggested answers or completions. Select the one that BEST answers the question or completes the statement. *PRINT THE LETTER OF THE CORRECT ANSWER IN THE SPACE AT THE RIGHT.*

1. For a superior to use *consultative supervision* with his subordinates effectively, it is ESSENTIAL that he
    A. accept the fact that his formal authority will be weakened by the procedure
    B. admit that he does not know more than all his men together and that his ideas are not always best
    C. utilize a committee system so that the procedure is orderly
    D. make sure that all subordinates are consulted so that no one feels left out

1._____

2. The *grapevine* is an informal means of communication in an organization. The attitude of a supervisor with respect to the grapevine should be to
    A. ignore it since it deals mainly with rumors and sensational information
    B. regard it as a serious danger which should be eliminated
    C. accept it as a real line of communication which should be listened to
    D. utilize it for most purposes instead of the official line of communication

2._____

3. The supervisor of an office that must deal with the public should realize that planning in this type of work situation
    A. is useless because he does not know how many people will request service or what service they will request
    B. must be done at a higher level but that he should be ready to implement the results of such planning
    C. is useful primarily for those activities that are not concerned with public contact
    D. is useful for all the activities of the office, including those that relate to public contact

3._____

4. Assume that it is your job to receive incoming telephone calls. Those calls which you cannot handle yourself have to be transferred to the appropriate office.
If you receive an outside call for an extension line which is busy, the one of the following which you should do FIRST is to
    A. interrupt the person speaking on the extension and tell him a call is waiting
    B. tell the caller the line is busy and let him know every thirty seconds whether or not it is free
    C. leave the caller on "hold" until the extension is free
    D. tell the caller the line is busy and ask him if he wishes to wait

4._____

5. Your superior has subscribed to several publications directly related to your division's work, and he has asked you to see to it that the publications are circulated among the supervisory personnel in the division. There are eight supervisors involved.
The BEST method of insuring that all eight see these publications is to
   A. place the publication in the division's general reference library as soon as it arrives
   B. inform each supervisor whenever a publication arrives and remind all of them that they are responsible for reading it
   C. prepare a standard slip that can be stapled to each publication, listing the eight supervisors and saying, "Please read, initial your name, and pass along"
   D. send a memo to the eight supervisors saying that they may wish to purchase individual subscriptions in their own names if they are interested in seeing each issue

6. Your superior has telephoned a number of key officials in your agency to ask whether they can meet at a certain time next month. He has found that they can all make it, and he has asked you to confirm the meeting.
Which of the following is the BEST way to confirm such a meeting?
   A. Note the meeting on your superior's calendar.
   B. Post a notice of the meeting on the agency bulletin board.
   C. Call the officials on the day of the meeting to remind them of the meeting.
   D. Write a memo to each official involved, repeating the time and place of the meeting.

7. Assume that a new city regulation requires that certain kinds of private organizations file information forms with your department. You have been asked to write the short explanatory message that will be printed on the front cover of the pamphlet containing the forms and instructions.
Which of the following would be the MOST appropriate way of beginning this message?
   A. Get the readers' attention by emphasizing immediately that there are legal penalties for organizations that fail to file before a certain date.
   B. Briefly state the nature of the enclosed forms and the types of organizations that must file.
   C. Say that your department is very sorry to have to put organizations to such an inconvenience.
   D. Quote the entire regulation adopted by the city, even if it is quite long and is expressed din complicated legal language.

8. Suppose that you have been told to make up the vacation schedule for the 18 employees in a particular unit. In order for the unit to operate effectively, only a few employees can be on vacation at the same time.
Which of the following is the MOST advisable approach in making up the schedule?
   A. Draw up a schedule assigning vacations in alphabetical order
   B. Find out when the supervisors want to take their vacations, and randomly assign whatever periods are left to the non-supervisory personnel

C. Assign the most desirable times to employees of longest standing and the least desirable times to the newest employees
D. Have all employees state their own preference, and then work out any conflicts in consultation with the people involved

9. Assume that you have been asked to prepare job descriptions for various positions in your department.
Which of the following are the basic points that should be covered in a *job description*?
   A. General duties and responsibilities of the position, with examples of day-to-day tasks
   B. Comments on the performances of present employees
   C. Estimates of the number of openings that may be available in each category during the coming year
   D. Instructions for carrying out the specific tasks assigned to your department

9.____

10. Of the following, the biggest DISADVANTAGE in allowing a free flow of communications in an agency is that such a free flow
    A. decreases creativity
    B. increases the use of the *grapevine*
    C. lengthens the chain of command
    D. reduces the executive's power to direct the flow of information

10.____

11. A downward flow of authority in an organization is one example of _____ communication.
    A. horizontal   B. informal   C. circular   D. vertical

11.____

12. Of the following, the one that would MOST likely block effective communication is
    A. concentration only on the issues at hand
    B. lack of interest or commitment
    C. use of written reports
    D. use of charts and graphs

12.____

13. An ADVANTAGE of the *lecture* as a teaching tool is that it
    A. enables a person to present his ideas to a large number of people
    B. allows the audience to retain a maximum of the information given
    C. holds the attention of the audience for the longest time
    D. enables the audience member to easily recall the main points

13.____

14. An ADVANTAGE of the *small-group* discussion as a teaching tool is that
    A. it always focuses attention on one person as the leader
    B. it places collective responsibility on the group as a whole
    C. its members gain experience by summarizing the ideas of others
    D. each member of the group acts as a member of a team

14.____

15. The one of the following that is an ADVANTAGE of a *large-group* discussion, when compared to a small-group discussion, is that the large-group discussion
    A. moves along more quickly than a small-group discussion
    B. allows its participants to feel more at ease, and speak out more freely
    C. gives the whole group a chance to exchange ideas on a certain subject at the same occasion
    D. allows its members to feel a greater sense of personal responsibility

15._____

KEY (CORRECT ANSWERS)

1.	D	6.	D	11.	D
2.	C	7.	B	12.	B
3.	D	8.	D	13.	A
4.	D	9.	A	14.	D
5.	C	10.	D	15.	C

EXAMINATION SECTION

TEST 1

DIRECTIONS: Each question or incomplete statement is followed by several suggested answers or completions. Select the one that BEST answers the question or completes the statement. *PRINT THE LETTER OF THE CORRECT ANSWER IN THE SPACE AT THE RIGHT.*

1. Managing conflict effectively by avoiding no-win situations, positively influencing the actions of others and using _____ strategies are what make a great leader.
   A. persuasive   B. ambiguous   C. prosecution   D. performance

   1._____

2. In today's business world, collaboration will bring together people from distinct backgrounds. These collaborative groups may not share common norms, morals or _____, but they can offer unique _____.
   A. vocabulary; perspectives
   B. salaries; vocabulary
   C. modifications; insights
   D. perspectives; salaries

   2._____

3. E-mail is a great tool for communication; however, which of the following should you be careful of when in electronic communication with a colleague?
   A. Font size
   B. E-mail length
   C. Font color
   D. Tone of voice

   3._____

4. A formal relationship can BEST be described as
   A. regulated by procedures or directives
   B. personal and relaxed
   C. emotionally distant and very uncomfortable
   D. confusing and unproductive

   4._____

5. John is in a meeting with his supervisor ad coworkers. He is thinking about what he's going to have for dinner that night when his boss asks him a question. John can repeat back what his supervisor said, but he cannot retain what was said during the meeting.
   This is a classic example of failing to
   A. focus at work
   B. effectively listen
   C. leave personal plans outside the workplace
   D. care about meetings

   5._____

6. A person's choice of _____ can directly affect communication.
   A. clothing   B. food   C. hygiene   D. words

   6._____

7. Why is it important to relax when communicating with team members?
   A. Relaxing always means having better ideas.
   B. People will automatically like you more if you are relaxed.

   7._____

C. If you are nervous, you may talk too quickly and make it hard for others to understand your message or directive.
D. No one likes someone who is always working, so it is important to relax and not work too hard.

8. In order to show you are genuinely interested in what others have to say, you should
   A. tell them how nice they are
   B. repeat what they say back to them
   C. nod and find something to compliment them about
   D. ask questions and seek clarification from them

9. Jack and James are always arguing with one another. Their supervisor calls each one in separately to talk to them. He asks Jack to think about things from James' point of view and he asks James to do the same for Jack.
   What is the supervisor trying to get each person to do?
   A. Get along   B. Be positive
   C. Communicate effectively   D. Empathize

10. When working in groups, disagreements
    A. should be avoided at all costs
    B. are often a healthy way of building understanding and camaraderie
    C. lead coworkers to hate one another and the company they work for
    D. don't happen if the supervisor chooses the right people to work together

11. If things go wrong in a group situation, it is important to AVOID
    A. the boss   B. disagreements or arguments
    C. scapegoating   D. being polite and fair to one another

12. If you are a listener who likes to hear the rationale behind a message, your listening style would be described as _____ style.
    A. results   B. process   C. reasons   D. eye contact

13. Which of the following BEST describes a psychological barrier in communication?
    A. Molly is so stressed about her paying for her mortgage that she can't focus at work right now.
    B. John doesn't understand a lot of the terms the IT specialist used in an e-mail sent out to everyone.
    C. Jerry is a little older and has a hard time hearing everything so sometimes he misses parts of a conversation.
    D. Linda doesn't want to be at the company for longer than a few months, so she doesn't really try too hard to fit in.

14. Body language, also known as _____, is really important when building rapport with coworkers and communicating effectively.
    A. verbal language   B. kinesthetic
    C. non-verbal communication   D. facial expressions

15. Which of the following might be a good example of someone who has a "closed" posture?
    A. Hands are apart on the arms of the chair.
    B. His/her arms are folded.
    C. They are directly facing you.
    D. They barely speak above a whisper.

16. Which of the following can eye contact be used for?
    A. To give and receive feedback
    B. To let someone know when it is their turn to speak
    C. To communicate how you feel about someone
    D. All of the above

17. Which of the following is NOT a form of non-verbal communication?
    A. Crossing your arms when talking to someone
    B. Using space within the room in a conversation
    C. Clearing your throat before you speak]
    D. Saying "10-4" when asked if you understand

18. Your best friend has just been hired at the company you work for. You notice he has come into work on several occasions after staying out late the night before. His work has not suffered yet, but you fear it will.
    Which of the following actions should you take to help prevent future problems?
    A. Do nothing; he's your friend but it is his life
    B. Try to talk to him and help him see the importance of not creating bad habits.
    C. Talk to your supervisor and tell him your friend isn't suitable for the job
    D. Tell your friend to change his ways or to quit

19. Interacting with coworkers can be positively or negatively affected by _____ when someone's previous biases and assumptions shape their reactions in future situations.
    A. racism   B. past experience
    C. interpersonal skills D. active listening

20. Which of the following scenarios BEST describes a person who is being subjective?
    A. Sally is fair and honest when she listens to coworkers. She does not take sides and wants the best solution to the problem.
    B. Mike doesn't like Steve, because he thinks Steve is only out for himself. Still, Steve offers valuable insights, so Mike tries not to let personal feelings get in the way of working together.
    C. Jamie is dating Veronica's ex and Veronica just found out. Now, Veronica immediately shoots down anything Jamie suggests during a meeting as irrational and superfluous.
    D. None of the above

21. Which important communications tem is MOST closely defined as "the quality of a sound governed by the rate of vibrations producing it; the degree of highness or lowness of a tone"?
    A. Tone
    B. Pitch
    C. Effective communication
    D. Rationalization

    21.____

22. _____ is when a person tries to make an imprudent and reckless action seem reasonable.
    A. Projection
    B. Self-deception
    C. Past experience
    D. Rationalization

    22.____

23. When holding conversations with coworkers, you should
    A. do most of the talking
    B. let others do most of the talking
    C. try to split time between talking and listening
    D. zone out and wait for the meeting to finish

    23.____

24. A new hire just arrived and you are meeting her for the first time. Which of the following actions is MOST appropriate?
    A. Walk up and introduce yourself with a smile and a handshake
    B. Wait for her to come and introduce herself
    C. Approach her and offer a hug to make her feel welcome
    D. Ignore the new hire; she is likely your competition

    24.____

25. If you are the type of listener who likes to discuss concepts or issues in detail, you would MOST likely fall under which listening style?
    A. Process
    B. Reasons
    C. Results
    D. None of the above

    25.____

KEY (CORRECT ANSWERS)

1.	A	11.	C
2.	A	12.	C
3.	D	13.	A
4.	A	14.	C
5.	B	15.	B
6.	D	16.	D
7.	C	17.	D
8.	D	18.	B
9.	D	19.	B
10.	B	20.	C

21. B
22. D
23. C
24. A
25. A

TEST 2

DIRECTIONS: Each question or incomplete statement is followed by several suggested answers or completions. Select the one that BEST answers the question or completes the statement. *PRINT THE LETTER OF THE CORRECT ANSWER IN THE SPACE AT THE RIGHT.*

1. Which of the following is an example of the BEST practice when communicating in the workplace?
   A. You are horrible with remembering names so you try to use nicknames to cover up for your poor memory.
   B. You only pay attention to the names of people who you work for or who you deem to be "important."
   C. You try to remember everyone's names and use them whenever possible.
   D. None of the above

    1._____

2. Words of civility such as "please" and "thank you" should be used _____ when conversing with coworkers and business partners.
   A. always   B. sometimes   C. rarely   D. never

    2._____

3. When communicating with others, one should _____ stand as close to them as possible and make body contact in order to get an important point across.
   A. always   B. sometimes   C. rarely   D. never

    3._____

4. The MOST appropriate way to end a conversation is to
   A. seek a mutual resolution, but leave abruptly if it continues
   B. find a way to wrap up the conversation so the other person knows it is time to move on
   C. look impatient so hopefully the person will get the hint
   D. tell the other person the conversation should end

    4._____

5. Another name for interpersonal communication in an office setting is
   A. peer-to-peer communication   B. mass communication
   C. virtual reality   D. e-mailing

    5._____

6. Of the following statements, choose the one you feel is the MOST correct.
   A. Devoid of interpersonal communication, people become sick.
   B. Communication is not completely needed for humans.
   C. People are the only animals that need to have relationships in order to survive.
   D. Important communication is not really relevant until after you become an adult.

    6._____

7. John is giving a presentation on ways to communicate effectively with peers. He is having trouble deciding on what to say in his speech.
   Which of the following statements should he AVOID using?
   A. Always try to understand another person's point of view or perspective
   B. Try to imagine what someone is going to say before they actually say it

    7._____

C. Be aware of how non-verbal cues like eye contact and body language affect how your message is received
D. Both B and C

8. Which of the following would MOST affect our perception of communication with coworkers?
   A. Past experiences
   B. Marital problems
   C. Rumors spread about coworkers
   D. None of the above

9. Many people think of communication as both _____ and _____ messages.
   A. formal; informal
   B. hearing; listening
   C. sending; receiving
   D. finding; decoding

10. Why is context important in communication?
    A. It's important to know which buttons to push in order to get what you want.
    B. Saying something to one person may not have the same effect as saying it to someone else.
    C. Context is only important if you are worried about what others think.
    D. None of the above

11. If your brother is normally bright and talkative during the summer, but you notice he gets quiet and subdued in the winter, the MOST likely communication context he is dealing with would be
    A. relational   B. cultural   C. inner   D. physical

12. _____ is an example of a negative nonverbal action you can take.
    A. Smiling
    B. Using a tone of voice that matches your message
    C. Maintaining eye contact
    D. Slumping your shoulders

13. Cultural context can BEST be described as
    A. what people think of as it relates to the event they are participating in (i.e., wedding versus a funeral)
    B. the connection between a father and his son
    C. rules and patterns of Americans versus the Japanese
    D. thoughts, feelings, and sensations inside a person's head

14. Which of the following BEST describes feedback?
    A. Staring at the speaker while he talks
    B. Nodding and smiling while listening to a speaker
    C. Standing an appropriate distance away so the speaker does not get uncomfortable
    D. Trying to speak while the other person is speaking because you have something more important to say

15. Being able to communicate more effectively can be improved upon by
    A. continually making an effort to be as flexible as possible when talking to others
    B. committing to one style of speaking until you master it
    C. using the same style of correspondence as the person with whom you are speaking
    D. always using the opposite style of communication from the person you are speaking to

16. John walks up to Sally and compliments her on the dress she wore to work today. In his mind, John was just being friendly, but Sally went to her manager and filed a harassment charge against John.
    This miscommunication could MOST easily be classified as an error in what?
    A. Reality   B. Perception   C. Friendship   D. Loyalty

17. If a speaker's tone is flat and monotone, which of the following is the MOST likely reaction that listeners will have?
    They will
    A. enthused by the message
    B. enjoy the message but not be overly excited about it
    C. be polite and interested but will not seem very engaged
    D. be bored and uninterested in the message

18. When Steve speaks to his group about his ideas, he generally has a higher pitch to his voice and gesticulates frequently.
    This lead his team members to believe that Steve
    A. is enthusiastic and has great ideas for the group
    B. has had too much caffeine and needs to relax
    C. is trying to show off for the boss and make them look bad
    D. is extremely smart and great at his job

19. _____ is used when a person wants to add stress to key words in communication. It lets the audience understand the mood or feelings of particular words or phrases.
    A. Anger   B. Tone   C. Perception   D. Inflection

20. If Barry tells Bill that his haircut looks "great" and Bill can tell Barry is being insincere, which of the following tones is Barry MOST likely using?
    A. Affectionate   B. Apologetic   C. Threatening   D. Sarcastic

21. As a supervisor, it is important that everyone clearly comprehends everything you communicate to them.
    In order to ensure this happens, which of the following things should you avoid?
    A. Overusing jargon
    B. Explaining something more than once
    C. Speaking slowly and annunciating everything
    D. Having meetings in the morning

22. If your supervisor is looking down at the ground or has his back to you as he is speaking, it MOST clearly indicates to those who are listening to him that the supervisor
    A. is shy and doesn't like speaking in front of people
    B. is disinterested and doesn't care what he's talking about
    C. is approachable and friendly
    D. dislikes his job and wants to get out as soon as possible

    22.____

23. Interpersonal communication helps you
    A. know what others are thinking
    B. turn into an inspiring speaker, especially in public
    C. learn about yourself
    D. communicate with the general public

    23.____

24. In general, people who smile more are perceived as
    A. devious   B. friendly
    C. attractive   D. easy to manipulate

    24.____

25. If your supervisor constantly takes advantage of you and expresses his or her opinion often at the expense of you or other workers, which communication style are they MOST likely using?
    A. Nonassertive   B. Assertive   C. Aggressive   D. Peacemaking

    25.____

KEY (CORRECT ANSWERS)

1.	C		11.	D
2.	A		12.	D
3.	D		13.	C
4.	B		14.	B
5.	A		15.	A
6.	A		16.	B
7.	B		17.	D
8.	A		18.	A
9.	C		19.	D
10.	B		20.	D

21.	A
22.	B
23.	D
24.	B
25.	C

EXAMINATION SECTION
TEST 1

DIRECTIONS: Each question or incomplete statement is followed by several suggested answers or completions. Select the one that BEST answers the question or completes the statement. PRINT THE LETTER OF THE CORRECT ANSWER IN THE SPACE AT THE RIGHT.

1. You attend a meeting where contentious issues will come up. To avoid any negative behavior, what should be done at the beginning of the gathering?
    A. Each side of the controversial issues should be heard
    B. A moderator should tell everyone that they do not expect to have both sides come to an agreement
    C. A neutral team member should make sure everyone agrees on facts involved with the problem
    D. Make sure your own side is heard before the other side gets a chance to speak

1._____

2. E-mail is a large part of business communication. However, many e-mails are confusing or contain mistakes that lead to misunderstandings and misinterpretation. Of every 100 business-related e-mails, approximately how many are misunderstood by recipients?
    A. 10
    B. 20
    C. 50
    D. 90

2._____

3. Which of the following is a disadvantage of using e-mail when communicating with employees?
    A. It is hard to put details into e-mails
    B. You cannot send them out to large groups of people
    C. It is quicker to hold a meeting than send out an e-mail
    D. It can be easy to misinterpret the tone of an e-mail

3._____

4. In the communication process, a receiver is
    A. the person encoding a message
    B. a message pathway
    C. the person who decodes a message
    D. interference within a message

4._____

5. One of your clients calls you and asks you to explain a confusing bylaw in one of his policies. What is the appropriate way to respond to him?
    A. Immediately transfer him to your manager
    B. Tell him to check the policy on your company's website
    C. Explain the policy in simpler terms and e-mail him a copy of the written policy
    D. Mail him a printed copy of the policy and tell him to read it for himself

5._____

6. Your boss asks you to give a presentation to your coworkers. How can you make sure they will remember the important parts of your production?
   A. Make sure your visual aids are "attention getters"
   B. Make humorous statements when you want the audience to remember something
   C. Allow the audience to ask questions about the important aspects of the presentation
   D. Summarize and stress your main ideas

6._____

7. Which of the following is important to keep in mind when preparing to make a presentation?
   A. Audience interest and perspective
   B. Visual aids
   C. Charts and graphs
   D. Audience size

7._____

8. Why is customer feedback important to a company?
   A. It tells you if you are popular or not
   B. It lets you know if additional training is needed in certain areas
   C. It can help your company realize whether corporate policies need to be changed or not
   D. It informs you how the public feels about your company's ability to meet their needs

8._____

9. Your organization issued a press release and it is your job to post it on the website for public viewing. This might require basic knowledge of
   A. Windows   B. FTP   C. HTML   D. HP

9._____

10. The managing director at your firm just made a significant error during his keynote speech at a prestigious conference. This flawed statement could mean a noteworthy loss to investors and other businesses. How should Public Relations BEST handle this misstep?
    A. E-mail the corrected statement to anyone who attended the conference
    B. Put the corrected statement up on the company's website
    C. Train all Public Relations employees to answer questions about the issue
    D. Have the director publicly make a statement correcting his error and apologizing for the incorrect information

10._____

11. In order to meet deadlines, a supervisor should
    A. schedule work and stay informed on the progress of each task
    B. make sure he or she delegates the work properly
    C. hire temps when projects start to overwhelm regular staff
    D. have a good idea how capable each of your reliable employees are

11._____

12. One of your clients continually calls and complains that your staff members are "a bunch of idiots" and a constant source of frustration.
What is the BEST way to deal with this situation?
    A. Keep quiet and let your client continue to rant until she calms down
    B. Tell her you will not speak to her until she stops using derogatory language toward your staff
    C. Attempt to steer the conversation towards the actual issue your client is having
    D. Tell your client they will need to speak with your manager

12._____

13. Your staff meetings constantly devolve into coworkers trying to push different agendas and, as a result, nothing productive gets done. Your manager asks you for input on how to solve this problem. What should she do?
    A. Tell all members to consider opening up to other priorities if they are logical
    B. Acknowledge the various opinions but attempt to focus on common goals and interests first
    C. Pretend everyone is on the same page and force everyone to get along or threaten them with termination
    D. Begin by allowing each member to speak about their priority then have everyone vote on which issues should be handled first

13._____

14. You go into a loan office to procure a loan of $1,000. They offer you the loan with a 6% yearly interest. If you plan on paying off the loan in exactly one year, how much will you pay back for the loan?
    A. $1,160.00   B. $1,016.67   C. $1,060.00   D. $166.67

14._____

15. You want to respond quickly to a client that is thinking about leaving for another company's services. What is the FIRST thing you should do?
    A. Prepare an outline of what you want to say
    B. Brainstorm on possible reasons why they might want to leave
    C. Call them immediately and demand to know why they want to leave
    D. Decide on the approach that would be best to take with the customer to retain their loyalty

15._____

16. You are at a convention delivering a speech to company stakeholders. During the Q&A session, one stakeholder makes a suggestion you think is practical and valuable. How should you respond?
    A. Tell him the idea is worthwhile and promise to bring it to the appropriate person's attention
    B. Tell him it's a good idea and move on
    C. Tell him it's a good idea but you are not the person to talk to about it
    D. Tell him that someone in your company probably thought of that idea a long time ago

16._____

17. Sarah has the skills to do her job but her project teammates complain that she is not working hard and therefore isn't doing her share.
The best response is to
    A. explain to her the standards and expectations of the job
    B. put her with a different team to see if anything changes
    C. give her a firm reprimand and tell her to get her act together
    D. fire her – you'll find someone else who won't take the job for granted

17._____

18. Which of the following would NOT be considered verbal communication?
    A. E-mail exchange
    B. Listening
    C. Telephone calls
    D. Text messaging

18._____

19. Feedback from a large number of customers indicates that many features of the company website do not function as intended and are confusing in nature. After reviewing the web features for yourself, you determine that the complaints are accurate. What is the MOST appropriate immediate action to take?
    A. Set up a meeting between tech/web services and other necessary departments to determine what changes need to be made and when
    B. Inform the customers that the company is aware of the problems and will implement changes in next year's scheduled website update
    C. Demand an explanation from web services and an immediate overhaul of the website
    D. Provide customers with the name and phone number of a support contact

19._____

20. Which form of communication would be optimal if you wanted to talk to your offices in Ireland, France and China at the same time?
    A. Video-conferencing
    B. Presentation
    C. Report
    D. E-mail

20._____

21. Which size of business is most likely to use informal communication more regularly?
    A. Medium
    B. Large
    C. Small
    D. International

21._____

22. E-mails are effective when used to
    A. send long, complex information
    B. avoid confrontation
    C. exchange ideas
    D. discuss sensitive issues

22._____

23. If a customer calls needing someone to explain a policy that is complex in nature, and you don't have the specific answers they are looking for, what should you do?

    A. Give them as good of an answer as you can provide and hope that is enough
    B. Ask them to give you some time to find all the relevant information and tell them you'll call them back when you do
    C. Refer the caller to another more informed employee even if it means they will switch to that employee in the future
    D. Pretend to know the answers even if it means misleading your customer

23._____

24. Which of the following does NOT involve workplace communication?

    A. Answering customer letters
    B. Listening to instructions
    C. Lifting heavy boxes
    D. Working on team projects

24._____

25. Why is it important that one person does not dominate discussion during team meetings?

    A. They may ramble which would make the meeting unbearably long
    B. Other team members may not get the chance to give their input
    C. Some members may lose focus and begin to daydream
    D. No one wants to hear the same voice for any length of time

25._____

KEY (CORRECT ANSWERS)

1. B	11. A	21. C
2. C	12. C	22. A
3. D	13. A	23. C
4. C	14. C	24. C
5. C	15. D	25. B
6. D	16. A	
7. A	17. A	
8. D	18. B	
9. C	19. A	
10. D	20. A	

TEST 2

DIRECTIONS: Each question or incomplete statement is followed by several suggested answers or completions. Select the one that BEST answers the question or completes the statement. PRINT THE LETTER OF THE CORRECT ANSWER IN THE SPACE AT THE RIGHT.

1. If a customer calls for information about a policy that is run by a rival business, what is the BEST way to respond?
    A. Tell them to check the other company's website
    B. Clarify that you are not responsible for the policy and therefore cannot comment
    C. Refer the caller to the other agency's office number
    D. Give them information to the best of your ability

1._____

2. Which of the following is the MOST effective way to communicate during a speech?
    A. Prepare and memorize your script and stick to it throughout
    B. Speak with note cards you can reference throughout the speech
    C. Read the slides on your PowerPoint and try to make eye contact when you can
    D. Speak about whatever comes to your mind and don't worry about the note cards

2._____

3. Your boss wants to send a message to office employees about a social event. She should send out a(n)
    A. agenda
    B. notice
    C. report
    D. fax

3._____

4. Which of the following programs would be used to generate graphs and charts to be displayed in a public presentation?
    A. PowerPoint
    B. Photoshop
    C. Outlook
    D. Excel

4._____

5. What should any good speaker avoid while making a presentation?
    A. Controversial issues
    B. Jargon
    C. Anything to do with finances or graphs
    D. Customer policies and/or company goals

5._____

6. A new hire has been placed onto your team. What is the best way to help him succeed?
    A. Let him try things out on his own and aid him if he asks
    B. Provide mentoring to help him learn
    C. Give him specific and detailed direction so he will not make any mistakes
    D. Work with him side by side

7. What should a public speaker do if they are confronted with a question to which they don't have a good answer?
    A. Give an answer based on their comprehension of the topic
    B. Evade and try to focus the discussion on a topic you know better
    C. Tell them you have no idea how to answer the question
    D. Tell them you do not know the full answer to the question but you will find out and get back to them

8. Effective business communication
    A. decreases the number of positive responses to requests on the first try
    B. increases reading time
    C. increases the time it takes disagreements to surface
    D. builds a positive image of your business

9. A customer sends your company a nasty complaint letter and you are in charge of responding. What is the BEST way to begin your response?
    A. "I was given the task of replying to your complaint regarding our set of laws concerning Item #665349."
    B. "This is a letter to tell you we got your complaint concerning new policies on returns in regards to the item in question."
    C. "Hi, I am really glad you sent in your letter of complaint telling us what's wrong with our policies in connection with Item #665349."
    D. "Thank you for expressing your dissatisfaction with new policies in connection with your purchase (Item #665349)."

10. You are getting ready to write a memo correcting a fault made by your team. Which of the following MUST be included in the letter?
    A. Details of why the error occurred
    B. A clear idea of exactly which team member is responsible for the fault
    C. Explanation of how this error will be fixed
    D. Excuses about how it is not really your team's fault because they are doing the best they can

11. Company X announced on its website that sales this year increased by 112%. If sales last year were $500,000, what amount are sales this year?
    A. $512,000
    B. $560,000
    C. $1.06 million
    D. $1.6 million

12. Your boss wants to implement policy changes that could be unpopular among coworkers. He asks you how to best introduce these changes. What should you tell him?
    A. He should let people know what is happening and ask if they have feedback
    B. He should announce the policy changes without any warning and make it clear that employees need to accept the changes and adapt
    C. He should allow each employee to vote on all the separate policy changes. The only policy changes that will happen will be the ones that receive a majority vote.
    D. None of the above

13. If you ever have an irate customer who uses inflammatory language laced with obscenities, what is the BEST action to take?
    A. Tell them they need to calm down or you will discontinue the conversation
    B. Immediately transfer the call to your manager
    C. Let the customer finish his/her rant, then try to respond with a solution
    D. Hang up on the customer – your company doesn't need someone like that

14. Of the following, pick the one that doesn't fit with the others.
    A. Excel
    B. Gmail
    C. Yahoo
    D. Hotmail

15. Each person desires to be viewed positively by others, to be thought of favorably. This is referred to as maintaining
    A. positive face
    B. politeness
    C. abstraction
    D. negative face

16. A team member dominates every conversation she is involved in. As a team leader, how should you handle this situation?
    A. Refuse to let her speak until she learns how to listen
    B. Support other team members enthusiastically whenever they do speak up
    C. Stop the meeting and remind everyone to chip in with their opinions
    D. Privately discuss the issue with the team member in hopes of getting her to see why everyone should have a say

17. You are someone who gets really anxious when giving public speeches. Which of the following will NOT help you overcome your fears?
    A. Acknowledge your fears
    B. Avoid eye contact with audience members, that way it won't feel like they are there
    C. Act confident even if you don't feel it
    D. Channel your nervous energy into your speech

18. Which of the following would NOT be considered part of the setting for a public speech?   18._____
    A. Size of the audience
    B. Location of the speech
    C. If speech is held indoors or outdoors
    D. The length of the speech you're giving

19. Your boss tells you that a few of your employees have been complaining about your erratic methods of supervision. How should you respond?   19._____
    A. Tell your boss that you'll go to a supervisor training program
    B. Ask your boss if it was ethical for your employees to go over your head
    C. Ask your boss for specific acts that are considered inconsistent
    D. Explain that these few employees have made you inconsistent because of their neediness

20. Which of the following is NOT a purpose of giving a speech?   20._____
    A. To inform
    B. To entertain
    C. To persuade
    D. None of the above

21. Which of the following is an advantage of learning to effectively speak in public?   21._____
    A. Creating a message that can be understood by lots of people
    B. Convincing your audience of an important issue
    C. Inspiring your audience to take a certain action
    D. All of the above

22. Which of the following is NOT a reason that people fear speaking in public?   22._____
    A. They are perfectionists
    B. They are anxious about their future with the company
    C. They are overly prepared
    D. They tend to put off speech preparation until the last minute

23. Which of the following would be considered an external audience of a company?   23._____
    A. Peers
    B. Superiors
    C. Subordinates
    D. Stockholders

24. In preparation for a speech, what is important for you to know?   24._____
    A. The purpose of your speech
    B. The audience listening to your speech
    C. The time constraints of the speech
    D. All of the above

25. An employee in your department informs you that the company's monthly e-mail newsletter was sent out to customers and subscribers with incorrect information. As the head of the department, your first step in an effort to fix this mistake should be to
    A. identify the person responsible and demand that they correct it
    B. assign someone in the department the task of developing a follow-up e-mail assuring customers that this sort of mistake will not occur again in future newsletters
    C. assign someone in the department the task of developing a follow-up e-mail that points out the error and contains corrected information
    D. inform the staff that you will be the only person to create and distribute future newsletters

25._____

KEY (CORRECT ANSWERS)

1. D	11. C	21. D
2. B	12. A	22. C
3. B	13. C	23. D
4. D	14. A	24. D
5. B	15. A	25. C
6. B	16. D	
7. D	17. B	
8. D	18. D	
9. D	19. C	
10. C	20. D	

EXAMINATION SECTION
TEST 1

DIRECTIONS: Each question or incomplete statement is followed by several suggested answers or completions. Select the one that BEST answers the question or completes the statement. *PRINT THE LETTER OF THE CORRECT ANSWER IN THE SPACE AT THE RIGHT.*

1. A specialist is meeting with a panel of local community leaders to determine their perceptions about the effectiveness of a recent outreach program. The leaders seem unresponsive to the specialist's questions, looking at the floor or each other without directly answering the specialist's questions.
One strategy that might work to elicit the desired information would be to
   A. try to discern the hidden meaning of their silence
   B. adopt a mildly confrontational tone and remind them of what's at stake in the community
   C. keep asking open-ended questions and wait patiently for responses
   D. tell them to come back when they're ready to tell you their opinions

2. Each of the following statements about maintaining a community's attention is true, EXCEPT:
   A. The more challenging it is to pay attention to a message, the more likely it is that it will be attended to
   B. Listeners will be more motivated to pay attention if a speech is personally meaningful
   C. People will be more likely to attend if a speaker pauses to suggest natural transitions in a speech
   D. Listeners will attend to messages that stand out

3. Each of the following is a key strategy to integrative bargaining among community members in conflict, EXCEPT
   A. focusing on positions, rather than interests
   B. separating the people from the problem
   C. aiming for an outcome based on an objectively identified standard
   D. using active listening skills, such as rephrasing and questioning

4. Which of the following is NOT one of the major variables to take into account when considering a community needs assessment?
   A. State of program development   B. Resources available
   C. Demographics   D. Community attitudes

5. Which of the following groups would probably be formed specifically for, or be involved in, the purpose of addressing a specific unmet community need?
   A. An existing consumer group
   B. A council of community representatives
   C. A committee
   D. An existing community organization

6. If a public outreach campaign designed to mobilize a community fails, the MOST likely reason for this failure is that the campaign
   A. was not specific about what it wanted people to do
   B. was overly serious and did not appeal to people's sense of humor
   C. offered no incentive for the audience to make a change
   D. did not use language that appealed to the audience's emotions

7. Nationwide, the rate of involvement of elderly people in community-based programs demonstrates that they are
   A. under-served when compared to other age groups
   B. served at about the same rate as other age groups
   C. over-served when compared to other age groups
   D. hardly served at all

8. In projecting the likelihood of an education program's success, a domestic violence specialist identifies every single event that must occur to complete the project. The specialist then arranges these events in sequential order and allocates time requirements for each. Finally, the total time is calculated and a model showing all their events and timelines is charted.
   The specialist has used
   A. a PERT chart   B. a simulation
   C. a Markov model   D. the critical path method

9. When working with members of a predominantly African-American community, specialists from other cultural backgrounds should be aware that African-Americans tend to express thoughts and feelings through descriptions of
   A. physically tangible sensations   B. problems to be analyzed
   C. corresponding analogies   D. spiritual issues

10. Local nonprofessionals should be considered useful to a specialist who is looking to undertake a community outreach or educational initiative.
    Which of the following is LEAST likely to be a characteristic or role demonstrated by these community members?
    A. Undertaking support functions at the agency
    B. Serving as a communication channel between the agency and clients
    C. Encouraging greater agency acceptance and credibility within the community
    D. Helping the agency to accomplish meaningful change

11. In working with Native American groups or clients, it is important to recognize that the GREATEST health problem facing their communities today is
    A. domestic violence   B. depression and suicide
    C. alcoholism   D. tuberculosis

3 (#1)

12. A specialist is facilitating a cooperative conflict resolution session between community members who have different opinions about what kinds of intervention services should be offered by the local adult protective services agency.
    Which of the following is NOT a guideline that should be followed in this process?
    A. Early in the negotiations, ask each party to name the issues on which they will positively not yield.
    B. Try to get the parties to view the issue from other points of view, beside the two or three conflicting ones.
    C. Have each side volunteer what it would be willing to do to resolve the conflict.
    D. At the end of the session, draw up a formal agreement with agreed-upon actions for both parties.

12.____

13. A specialist wants to evaluate the effectiveness of a local women's shelter. The shelter has suffered from lax participation, given the number of women who have been abused in the surrounding area. The specialist wants to speak with the women in the community who did not follow up on referrals to the shelter, and begins by visiting some of these women. After gaining the trust of these women, the specialist asks for the names of women they know who might be in need of help with a domestic violence situation.
    The specialist's approach in this case is _____ sampling.
    A. maximum variation   B. snowball
    C. convenience   D. typical case

13.____

14. When it comes to perceiving messages, people typically DON'T
    A. tend to simplify causal connections and sometimes even seek a single cause to explain what may be a highly complex effect
    B. tend to perceive messages independently of a categorical framework, especially if the message may be distorted by such an interpretation
    C. have a predisposition toward accepting any pattern that a speaker offers to explain seemingly unconnected facts
    D. tend to interpret things in the way they are viewed by their reference group

14.____

15. The elder members of Native American communities, regardless of kinship, are MOST commonly referred to as
    A. the ancients   B. father or mother
    C. grandfather or grandmother D. chiefs

15.____

16. Each of the following is typically an objective of community mobilization, EXCEPT:
    A. To convince existing community resources to alter their services or work together to address an unmet need
    B. To gather and distribute information to consumers and agencies about unmet needs

16.____

C. To publicize existing community resources and make them more accessible
D. To bring an unmet community need to public attention in order to achieve acceptance of and support for fulfilling the need

17. Research in community outreach shows that women often build friendships through shared positive feelings, whereas men often build friendships through
    A. metacommunication
    B. catharsis
    C. impression management
    D. shared activities

    17.____

18. Typically, the FIRST step in a community-needs assessment is to
    A. identify community's strengths
    B. explore the nature of the neighborhood
    C. get to know the area and its residents
    D. talk to people in the community

    18.____

19. Most public relations experts agree that _____ exposure(s) to a message is the minimum just to get the message noticed. If the aim of a public outreach campaign is action or a change in behavior, the agency budget must plan for more exposures.
    A. one
    B. two
    C. three
    D. four

    19.____

20. In the program development/community liaison model of community work and public outreach, the PRIMARY constituency is considered to be
    A. community representatives and the service agency board or administrators
    B. elected officials, social agencies, and interagency organizations
    C. marginalized or oppressed population groups in a city or region
    D. residents of a neighborhood, parish or rural county

    20.____

21. Social or interpersonal problems in many African-American communities have their roots in
    A. personality deficits
    B. unresolved family conflicts
    C. poor communication
    D. external stressors

    21.____

22. A public outreach campaign should
    I. focus on short-term, measurable goals, rather than ultimate outcomes
    II. try to alter entrenched attitudes within a short time, with powerfully worded messages
    III. proceed in steps or phases, each of which lays out a mechanism that leads to the desired effect
    IV. ignore causes that led to a problem, and instead focus on solutions

    The CORRECT answer is:
    A. I and II
    B. II and III
    C. III only
    D. I, II, III and IV

    22.____

23. Research findings indicate that in listing preferences for helping professional attributes, individuals from culturally diverse groups are MOST likely to consider _____ as more important than _____.
    A. personality similarity; either race/ethnic similarity or attitude similarity
    B. therapist experience; any kind of similarity
    C. race/ethnic similarity; attitude similarity
    D. attitude similarity; race/ethnic similarity

24. Each of the following is considered to be an objective of community organization EXCEPT
    A. effecting changes in the distribution of decision-making power
    B. helping people develop and strengthen the traits of self-direction and cooperation
    C. effecting and maintaining the balance between needs and resources in a community
    D. helping people deal with their problems by developing alternative behaviors

25. A specialist is helping the adult protective services agency to design a public outreach campaign. The topic to be addressed is complex, public understanding is low, and most professionals at the agency feel that having more complete information might change the opinions of community members. Which method of pre-campaign research is probably MOST appropriate?
    A. Deliberative polling
    B. Attitude scales
    C. Surveys or questionnaires
    D. Focus groups

KEY (CORRECT ANSWERS)

1.	C	11.	C
2.	A	12.	A
3.	A	13.	B
4.	C	14.	B
5.	C	15.	C
6.	A	16.	B
7.	A	17.	D
8.	D	18.	B
9.	C	19.	C
10.	A	20.	A

21. D
22. C
23. D
24. D
25. A

TEST 2

DIRECTIONS: Each question or incomplete statement is followed by several suggested answers or completions. Select the one that BEST answers the question or completes the statement. *PRINT THE LETTER OF THE CORRECT ANSWER IN THE SPACE AT THE RIGHT.*

1. A specialist has been called in to resolve a dispute between two community leaders who have been arguing about the level of service needed within the community. The discussion has been going on for several hours when the specialist arrives, and both people seem to be upset.
After calming the two down and getting each of them to agree on a statement of the problem, the specialist should ask each person to
    A. summarize his or her argument in three main points
    B. explain why he or she became so upset
    C. clearly state, in objective terms, the position of the other in a form that meets with the other's approval
    D. identify the best alternative outcome, other than their presumed ideal

2. In evaluating the impact of a public outreach campaign, the _____ model can be used early in the campaign to address first impressions.
    A. exposure or advertising
    B. expert interview
    C. impact monitoring or process
    D. experimental or quasi-experimental

3. When trying to motivate an older population to take action on a community problem, it is helpful to remember that older people
    A. are more self-reliant in their decision-making than other members of the same family
    B. often need more time to decide than younger people
    C. are more likely than younger people to view community problems self-referentially
    D. tend to take a pragmatic, rather than philosophical, view of life

4. The method of group or community decision-making that is normally MOST time-consuming is
    A. majority opinion   B. consensus
    C. expert opinion   D. authority rule

5. A local adult protective services agency has identified one of the goals of its recent public outreach campaign to be the mobilization of activists.
The campaign should probably
    A. target neutral audiences
    B. home in on supporters
    C. stick to purely factual information
    D. try to persuade community fence-sitters

6. Research of Native American youths' perceptions of family concerns for their well-being has generally found that these youths
   A. have a high degree of uncertainty about their families' feelings toward them
   B. believe their families don't care about them
   C. believe that their mothers care a great deal about them, but their fathers don't
   D. believe their families care a great deal about them

7. A domestic violence specialist is developing a new outreach program for the local community. The specialist has defined the target problem, set program goals, and planned the actions that will take place as a result of the program. Most likely, the next step will be to
   A. evaluate the resources available to achieve program goals
   B. define and sequence the steps that will be taken to achieve program goals
   C. determine how the program will be evaluated
   D. decide how the program will operate

8. Elder: *I'm so glad to have someone to talk to, someone who really understands my problem.*
   Specialist: *It is nice to be able to talk to someone who will listen.*
   Elder: *That's for sure.*
   In the above exchange, what listening skill is evident in the underlined statement?
   A. Verbatim response   B. Paraphrasing
   C. Advising   D. Evaluation

9. Which of the following activities is involved in the specialist's task of mobilizing?
   A. Meeting individuals in the community with problems and assisting them in finding help
   B. Identifying unmet community needs
   C. Speaking out against an unjust policy or procedure
   D. Developing new services or linking presently available services to meet community needs

10. The preliminary research associated with a public outreach campaign should FIRST be aimed at determining
    A. the budget
    B. the message's ultimate audience
    C. what media to use
    D. the short-term behavioral goals of the campaign

11. A specialist in a low-income community wants to plan programs that will deal with the influence of unemployment on domestic disturbances. The specialist needs to know not only how many unemployed people are in the community now, but also how many people will be unemployed at any particular tie in the future, and how those numbers will vary given certain conditions.

Probably the BEST way to trace employment rates over time and within differing conditions is through the use of
A. the critical path
B. linear programming
C. difference equations
D. the Markov model

12. Generally, public outreach programs—whatever their stated goal—should
   I. create a sense of urgency about a problem
   II. decline to identify opponents of the issue or idea
   III. propose concrete, easily understandable solutions
   IV. urge a specific action

   The CORRECT answer is:
   A. I only
   B. I, III and IV
   C. II and III
   D. I, II, III and IV

13. Which of the following methods of community needs assessment relies to the GREATEST degree on existing public records?
   A. Social indicators
   B. Field study
   C. Rates under treatment
   D. Key informant

14. During an interview with a Native American client, a specialist is careful to maintain close and nearly constant eye contact.
   The client is MOST likely to interpret this as a(n)
   A. show of high concern
   B. sign of disrespect
   C. uncomfortable assumption of intimacy
   D. attempt to intimidate

15. The BEST strategy for addressing an audience that is known to be captive, or even hostile, is to
   A. refer to experiences in common
   B. flatter the audience
   C. joke about things in or near the audience
   D. plead for fairness

16. Integrative conflict resolution is characterized by
   A. an overriding concern to maximize joint outcomes
   B. one side's interests opposing the other's
   C. a fixed and limited amount of resources to be divided, so that the more one group gets, the less another gets
   D. manipulation and withholding information as negotiation strategies

17. A specialist wants to learn how to interact with the members of a largely Latino community in a more culturally sensitive way.
   Which of the following is NOT a guideline for interacting with members of a Latino community?
   A. Efforts to foster independence and self-reliance may be interpreted by many Latinos as a lack of concern for others.
   B. Efforts to deal one-on-one with an adolescent client may serve to alienate the parents, especially the mother.

C. A nonverbal gesture, such as lowering the eyes, is interpreted by many Latinos as a sign of respect and deference to authority.
D. In much of Latino culture, the focus of control for problems tends to be much more external than internal.

18. Each of the following is a supporting assumption of community organization, EXCEPT:
    A. Democracy requires cooperative participation.
    B. In order for communities to change, it is necessary for each individual in the community to be willing to change.
    C. Communities often need help with organization and planning.
    D. Holistic approaches work better than fragmented or ad-hoc programs.

18._____

19. Helping professionals often have difficulty to bring community resources together to fulfill unmet community needs.
    Which of the following is NOT usually a reason for this?
    A. Some community groups resist assistance when it is offered.
    B. Few community groups make their needs known.
    C. Community resources frequently change the type of services they offer.
    D. Often, community resources prefer to work alone.

19._____

20. When dealing with groups or populations of elderly clients, specialists should be mindful that about _____ of the nation's elderly suffer from mental health problems.
    A. a tenth   B. a quarter   C. a third   D. half

20._____

21. In an African-American community, a specialist from another culture should recognize that church participation, for most African-Americans, is viewed as a
    A. method for maintaining control and communicating competency
    B. way of depersonalizing problems or troubles
    C. way to divert attention away from problems
    D. means of cathartic emotional release

21._____

22. Adult protective service programs supported by state statutes protect elderly people from abuse and neglect under the doctrine of
    A. parens patriae   B. habeas corpus
    C. in loco parentis   D. volenti non fit injuria

22._____

23. In terms of public outreach, which of the following statements about an audience is NOT generally true?
    A. The more heterogeneous the audience, the more necessary it will be to use specific examples and appeals to certain types of people.
    B. The smaller the audience, the more likely that its members will share assumptions and values.
    C. When the speaker does not know the status of an audience, it is best to assume that they are captive rather than voluntary.
    D. The larger an audience, the more formal a presentation is likely to be.

23._____

24. A specialist often spends time in the places frequented by community residents. She listens carefully to what residents seem most concerned about, and engages many in conversations, asking them how they see the problems in the community. During these conversations, she makes mental notes about whether the statements of the problems are the same things that are mentioned in their conversations. From these conversations, the worker determines what she thinks the unmet needs of the community are.
Which of the key issues in identifying unmet needs has the worker neglected to address?
    A. The different points of view regarding the issues, and whether there is any common ground
    B. Whether the stated problems and conversations with community residents reflect the same concerns
    C. How community residents define the issues
    D. What the residents talk about with one another in a community

24.____

25. Which of the following political styles should be used to promote an issue that could become controversial if it is perceived to involve major reforms?
    A. High-conflict, polarized
    B. High-conflict, consensual
    C. Moderate conflict, compromise-oriented
    D. Low-conflict, technical

25.____

KEY (CORRECT ANSWERS)

1.	C	11.	D
2.	A	12.	B
3.	B	13.	A
4.	B	14.	B
5.	B	15.	A
6.	D	16.	A
7.	A	17.	D
8.	B	18.	B
9.	D	19.	C
10.	B	20.	B

21.	D
22.	A
23.	A
24.	A
25.	D

EVALUATING CONCLUSIONS IN LIGHT OF KNOWN FACTS

An ability needed in many state jobs is the ability to decide if a conclusion is true, based on a set of facts. (These questions can also be called "Logic".) First read the facts (or premises) that are given, and then look at the conclusion. Assume the facts are true, and decide if the conclusion is:

1. Necessarily true.
2. Probably, but not necessarily true.
3. Indeterminable, cannot be determined.
4. Probably, but not necessarily false.
5. Necessarily false.

These five answer choices (above) are the same for each inference question.

1. FACTS: If the Commission approves the new proposal, the agency will move to a new location immediately. If the agency moves, five new supervisors will be appointed immediately. The Commission approved the new proposal.

    CONCLUSION: No new supervisors were appointed.

    1. Necessarily true.
    2. Probably, but not necessarily true.
    3. Indeterminable, cannot be determined.
    4. Probably, but not necessarily false.
    5. Necessarily false.

2. FACTS: If the director retires, John Jackson, the associate director, will not be transferred to another agency. Jackson will be promoted to director if he is not transferred. The director retired.

    CONCLUSION: Jackson will be promoted to director.

    1. Necessarily true.
    2. Probably, but not necessarily true.
    3. Indeterminable, cannot be determined.
    4. Probably, but not necessarily false.
    5. Necessarily false.

3. **FACTS:** If the maximum allowable income for food stamp recipients is increased, the number of food stamp recipients will increase. If the number of food stamp recipients increases, more funds must be allocated to the food stamp program, which will require a tax increase. Taxes cannot be raised without the approval of Congress. Congress probably will not approve a tax increase.

   CONCLUSION: The maximum allowable income for food stamp recipients will increase.

   1. Necessarily true.
   2. Probably, but not necessarily true.
   3. Indeterminable, cannot be determined.
   4. Probably, but not necessarily false.
   5. Necessarily false.

4. **FACTS:** If prices are raised and sales remain constant, profits will increase. Prices were raised and sales levels will probably be maintained.

   CONCLUSION: Profits will increase.

   1. Necessarily true.
   2. Probably, but not necessarily true.
   3. Indeterminable, cannot be determined.
   4. Probably, but not necessarily false.
   5. Necessarily false.

5. **FACTS:** Some employees in the personnel department are technicians. Most of the technicians working in the personnel department are test development specialists. Lisa Jones works in the personnel department.

   CONCLUSION: Lisa Jones is a technician.

   1. Necessarily true.
   2. Probably, but not necessarily true.
   3. Indeterminable, cannot be determined.
   4. Probably, but not necessarily false.
   5. Necessarily false.

INFERENCE QUESTION ANSWERS AND EXPLANATIONS

1. The correct answer is number 5 (necessarily false). The new proposal was approved. According to the facts, approval means that the agency will move, and moving to a new location means that five new supervisors will be appointed.

2. The correct answer is number 1 (necessarily true). According to the facts, the director retired, which means that Jackson will not be transferred and, therefore, will be promoted to director.

3. The correct answer is number 4 (probably, but not necessarily false). Since Congress probably will not approve a tax increase, the maximum allowable income for food stamp recipients probably will not increase.

4. The correct answer is number 2 (probably, but not necessarily true). According to the facts, profits will increase if prices are raised and sales remain constant. It is known that prices were raised. Although sales level will probably be maintained, this is not certain.

5. The correct answer is number 3 (indeterminable, cannot be determined). The facts give no indication of the proportion of employees who are technicians. Therefore, no conclusion can be drawn with respect to the probability that any one employee is a technician.

EVALUATING CONCLUSIONS IN LIGHT OF KNOWN FACTS
EXAMINATION SECTION
TEST 1

DIRECTIONS: Each question or incomplete statement is followed by several suggested answers or completions. Select the one that BEST answers the question or completes the statement. *PRINT THE LETTER OF THE CORRECT ANSWER IN THE SPACE AT THE RIGHT.*

Questions 1-9.

DIRECTIONS: In Questions 1 through 9, you will read a set of facts and a conclusion drawn from them. The conclusion may be valid or invalid, based on the facts—it's your task to determine the validity of the conclusion.

For each question, select the letter before the statement that BEST expresses the relationship between the given facts and the conclusion that has been drawn from them. Your choices are:
  A. The facts prove the conclusion;
  B. The facts disprove the conclusion; or
  C. The facts neither prove nor disprove the conclusion.

1. FACTS: If the supervisor retires, James, the assistant supervisor, will not be transferred to another department. James will be promoted to supervisor if he is not transferred. The supervisor retired.

   CONCLUSION: James will be promoted to supervisor.
   A. The facts prove the conclusion.
   B. The facts disprove the conclusion.
   C. The facts neither prove nor disprove the conclusion.

   1.____

2. FACTS: In the town of Luray, every player on the softball team works at Luray National Bank. In addition, every player on the Luray softball team wear glasses.

   CONCLUSIONS: At least some of the people who work at Luray National Bank wear glasses.
   A. The facts prove the conclusion.
   B. The facts disprove the conclusion.
   C. The facts neither prove nor disprove the conclusion.

   2.____

3. FACTS: The only time Henry and June go out to dinner is on an evening when they have childbirth classes. Their childbirth classes meet on Tuesdays and Thursdays.

   3.____

45

2 (#1)

CONCLUSION: Henry and June never go out to dinner on Friday or Saturday.
  A. The facts prove the conclusion.
  B. The facts disprove the conclusion.
  C. The facts neither prove nor disprove the conclusion.

4. FACTS: Every player on the field hockey team has at least one bruise. Everyone on the field hockey team also has scarred knees.

   CONCLUSION: Most people with both bruises and scarred knees are field hockey players.
     A. The facts prove the conclusion.
     B. The facts disprove the conclusion.
     C. The facts neither prove nor disprove the conclusion.

4.____

5. FACTS: In the chess tournament, Lance will win his match against Jane if Jane wins her match against Mathias. If Lance wins his match against Jane, Christine will not win her match against Jane.

   CONCLUSION: Christine will not win her match against Jane if Jane wins her match against Mathias.
     A. The facts prove the conclusion.
     B. The facts disprove the conclusion.
     C. The facts neither prove nor disprove the conclusion.

5.____

6. FACTS: No green lights on the machine are indicators for the belt drive status. Not all of the lights on the machine's upper panel are green. Some lights on the machine's lower panel are green.

   CONCLUSION: The green lights on the machine's lower panel may be indicators for the belt drive status.
     A. The facts prove the conclusion.
     B. The facts disprove the conclusion.
     C. The facts neither prove nor disprove the conclusion.

6.____

7. FACTS: At a small, one-room country school, there are eight students: Amy, Ben, Carla, Dan, Elliot, Francine, Greg, and Hannah. Each student is in either the 6th, 7th, or 8th grade. Either two or three students are in each grade. Amy, Dan, and Francine are all in different grades. Ben and Elliot are both in the 7th grade. Hannah and Carl are in the same grade.

   CONCLUSION: Exactly three students are in the 7th grade.
     A. The facts prove the conclusion.
     B. The facts disprove the conclusion.
     C. The facts neither prove nor disprove the conclusion.

7.____

8. FACTS: Two married couples are having lunch together. Two of the four people are German and two are Russian, but in each couple the nationality of the spouse is not necessarily the same as the other's. One person in the group is a teacher, the other a lawyer, one an engineer, and the other a writer. The teacher is a Russian man. The writer is Russian, and her husband is an engineer. One of the people, Mr. Stern, is German.

    CONCLUSION: Mr. Stern's wife is a writer.
    A. The facts prove the conclusion.
    B. The facts disprove the conclusion.
    C. The facts neither prove nor disprove the conclusion.

9. FACTS: The flume ride at the county fair is open only to children who are at least 36 inches tall. Lisa is 30 inches tall. John is shorter than Henry, but more than 10 inches taller than Lisa.

    CONCLUSION: Lisa is the only one who can't ride the flume ride.
    A. The facts prove the conclusion.
    B. The facts disprove the conclusion.
    C. The facts neither prove nor disprove the conclusion.

Questions 10-17.

DIRECTIONS: Questions 10 through 17 are based on the following reading passage. It is not your knowledge of the particular topic that is being tested, but your ability to reason based on what you have read. The passage is likely to detail several proposed courses of action and factors affecting these proposals. The reading passage is followed by a conclusion or outcome based on the facts in the passage, or a description of a decision taken regarding the situation. The conclusion is followed by a number of statements that have a possible connection to the conclusion. For each statement, you are to determine whether:
    A. The statement proves the conclusion.
    B. The statement supports the conclusion but does not prove it.
    C. The statement disproves the conclusion.
    D. The statement weakens the conclusion but does not disprove it.
    E. The statement has no relevance to the conclusion.

Remember that the conclusion after the passage is to be accepted as the outcome of what actually happened, and that you are being asked to evaluate the impact each statement would have had on the conclusion.

PASSAGE:

The Grand Army of Foreign Wars, a national veteran's organization, is struggling to maintain its National Home, where the widowed spouses and orphans of deceased members are housed together in a small village-like community. The Home is open to spouses and children who are bereaved for any reason, regardless of whether the member's death was related to military service, but a new global conflict has led to a dramatic surge in the number of members' deaths: many veterans who re-enlisted for the conflict have been killed in action.

The Grand Army of Foreign Wars is considering several options for handling the increased number of applications for housing at the National Home, which has been traditionally supported by membership due. At its national convention, it will choose only one of the following:

The first idea is a one-time $50 tax on all members, above and beyond the dues they pay already. Since the organization has more than a million member, this tax should be sufficient for the construction and maintenance of new housing for applicants on the existing grounds of the National Home. The idea is opposed, however, by some older members who live on fixed incomes. These members object in principle to the taxation of Grand Army members. The Grand Army has never imposed a tax on its members.

The second idea is to launch a national fundraising drive the public relations campaign that will attract donations for the National Home. Several national celebrities are members of the organization, and other celebrities could be attracted to the cause. Many Grand Army members are wary of this approach, however: in the past, the net receipts of some fundraising efforts have been relatively insignificant, given the costs of staging them.

A third approach, suggested by many of the younger members, is to have new applicants share some of the costs of construction and maintenance. The spouses and children would pay an up-front "enrollment" fee, based on a sliding scale proportionate to their income and assets, and then a monthly fee adjusted similarly to contribute to maintenance costs. Many older members are strongly opposed to this idea, as it is in direct contradiction to the principles on which the organization was founded more than a century ago.

The fourth option is simply to maintain the status quo, focus the organization's efforts on supporting the families who already live at the National Home, and wait to accept new applicants based on attrition.

CONCLUSION: At its annual national convention, the Grand Army of Foreign Wars votes to impose a one-time tax of $10 on each member for the purpose of expanding and supporting the National Home to welcome a larger number of applicants. The tax is considered to be the solution most likely to produce the funds needed to accommodate the growing number of applicants.

10. Actuarial studies have shown that because the Grand Army's membership consists mostly of older veterans from earlier wars, the organization's membership will suffer a precipitous decline in numbers in about five years.
    A. The statement proves the conclusion.
    B. The statement supports the conclusion but does not prove it.
    C. The statement disproves the conclusion.
    D. The statement weakens the conclusion but does not disprove it.
    E. The statement has no relevance to the conclusion.

10.____

11. After passage of the funding measure, a splinter group of older members appeals for the "sliding scale" provision to be applied to the tax, so that some members may be allowed to contribute less based on their income.
    A. The statement proves the conclusion.
    B. The statement supports the conclusion but does not prove it.
    C. The statement disproves the conclusion.
    D. The statement weakens the conclusion but does not disprove it.
    E. The statement has no relevance to the conclusion.

11.____

5 (#1)

12. The original charter of the Grand Army of Foreign Wars specifically states that the organization will not levy taxes or duties on its members beyond its modest annual dues. It takes a super-majority of attending delegates at the national convention to make alterations to the charter.
    A. The statement proves the conclusion.
    B. The statement supports the conclusion but does not prove it.
    C. The statement disproves the conclusion.
    D. The statement weakens the conclusion but does not disprove it.
    E. The statement has no relevance to the conclusion.

12._____

13. Six months before Grand Army of Foreign Wars' national convention, the Internal Revenue Service rules that because it is an organization that engages in political lobbying, the Grand Army must no longer enjoy its own federal tax-exempt status.
    A. The statement proves the conclusion.
    B. The statement supports the conclusion but does not prove it.
    C. The statement disproves the conclusion.
    D. The statement weakens the conclusion but does not disprove it.
    E. The statement has no relevance to the conclusion.

13._____

14. Two months before the national convention, Dirk Rockwell, arguably the country's most famous film actor, announces in a nationally televised interview that he has been saddened to learn of the plight of the National Home, and that he is going to make it his own personal crusade to see that it is able to house and support a greater number of widowed spouses and orphans in the future.
    A. The statement proves the conclusion.
    B. The statement supports the conclusion but does not prove it.
    C. The statement disproves the conclusion.
    D. The statement weakens the conclusion but does not disprove it.
    E. The statement has no relevance to the conclusion.

14._____

15. The Grand Army's final estimate is that the cost of expanding the National Home to accommodate the increased number of applicants will be about $61 million.
    A. The statement proves the conclusion.
    B. The statement supports the conclusion but does not prove it.
    C. The statement disproves the conclusion.
    D. The statement weakens the conclusion but does not disprove it.
    E. The statement has no relevance to the conclusion.

15._____

16. Just before the national convention, the Federal Department of Veterans Affairs announces steep cuts in the benefits package that is currently offered to the widowed spouses and orphans of veterans.
    A. The statement proves the conclusion.
    B. The statement supports the conclusion but does not prove it.
    C. The statement disproves the conclusion.
    D. The statement weakens the conclusion but does not disprove it.
    E. The statement has no relevance to the conclusion.

16._____

17. After the national convention, the Grand Army of Foreign Wars begins charging a modest "start-up" fee to all families who apply for residence at the national home.
    A. The statement proves the conclusion.
    B. The statement supports the conclusion but does not prove it.
    C. The statement disproves the conclusion.
    D. The statement weakens the conclusion but does not disprove it.
    E. The statement has no relevance to the conclusion.

Questions 18-25.

DIRECTIONS: Questions 18 through 25 each provide four factual statements and a conclusion based on these statements. After reading the entire question, you will decide whether:
   A. The conclusion is proved by statements I-IV;
   B. The conclusion is disproved by statements I-IV.
   C. The facts are not sufficient to prove or disprove the conclusion.

18. FACTUAL STATEMENTS:
    I. In the Field Day high jump competition, Martha jumped higher than Frank.
    II. Carl jumped higher than Ignacio.
    III. Ignacio jumped higher than Frank.
    IV. Dan jumped higher than Carl.

    CONCLUSION: Frank finished last in the high jump competition.
       A. The conclusion is proved by statements I-IV;
       B. The conclusion is disproved by statements I-IV.
       C. The facts are not sufficient to prove or disprove the conclusion.

19. FACTUAL STATEMENTS:
    I. The door to the hammer mill chamber is locked if light 6 is red.
    II. The door to the hammer mill chamber is locked only when the mill is operating.
    III. If the mill is not operating, light 6 is blue.
    IV. Light 6 is blue.

    CONCLUSION: The door to the hammer mill chamber is locked.
       A. The conclusion is proved by statements I-IV;
       B. The conclusion is disproved by statements I-IV.
       C. The facts are not sufficient to prove or disprove the conclusion.

20. FACTUAL STATEMENTS:
    I. Ziegfried, the lion tamer at the circus, has demanded ten additional minutes of performance time during each show.
    II. If Ziegfried is allowed his ten additional minutes per show, he will attempt to teach Kimba the tiger to shoot a basketball.
    III. If Kimba learns how to shoot a basketball, then Ziegfried was not given his ten additional minutes.
    IV. Ziegfried was given his ten additional minutes.

7 (#1)

CONCLUSION: Despite Ziegfried's efforts, Kimba did not learn how to shoot a basketball.
   A. The conclusion is proved by statements I-IV;
   B. The conclusion is disproved by statements I-IV.
   C. The facts are not sufficient to prove or disprove the conclusion.

21. FACTUAL STATEMENTS:
   I. If Stan goes to counseling, Sara won't divorce him.
   II. If Sara divorces Stan, she'll move back to Texas.
   III. If Sara doesn't divorce Stan, Irene will be disappointed.
   IV. Stan goes to counseling.

   CONCLUSION: Irene will be disappointed.
   A. The conclusion is proved by statements I-IV;
   B. The conclusion is disproved by statements I-IV.
   C. The facts are not sufficient to prove or disprove the conclusion.

22. FACTUAL STATEMENTS:
   I. If Delia is promoted to district manager, Claudia will have to be promoted to team leader.
   II. Delia will be promoted to district manager unless she misses her fourth-quarter sales quota.
   III. If Claudia is promoted to team leader, Thomas will be promoted to assistant team leader.
   IV. Delia meets her fourth-quarter sales quota.

   CONCLUSION: Thomas is promoted to assistant team leader.
   A. The conclusion is proved by statements I-IV;
   B. The conclusion is disproved by statements I-IV.
   C. The facts are not sufficient to prove or disprove the conclusion.

23. FACTUAL STATEMENTS:
   I. Clone D is identical to Clone B.
   II. Clone B is not identical to Clone A.
   III. Clone D is not identical to Clone C.
   IV. Clone E is not identical to the clones that are identical to Clone B.

   CONCLUSION: Clone E is identical to Clone D.
   A. The conclusion is proved by statements I-IV;
   B. The conclusion is disproved by statements I-IV.
   C. The facts are not sufficient to prove or disprove the conclusion.

24. FACTUAL STATEMENTS:
   I. In the Stafford Tower, each floor is occupied by a single business.
   II. Big G Staffing is on a floor between CyberGraphics and MainEvent.
   III. Gasco is on the floor directly below CyberGraphics and three floors above Treehorn Audio.
   IV. MainEvent is five floors below EZ Tax and four floors below Treehorn Audio.

8 (#1)

CONCLUSION: EZ Tax is on a floor between Gasco and MainEvent.
  A. The conclusion is proved by statements I-IV;
  B. The conclusion is disproved by statements I-IV.
  C. The facts are not sufficient to prove or disprove the conclusion.

25. FACTUAL STATEMENTS: 25.____
  I. Only county roads lead to Nicodemus.
  II. All the roads from Hill City to Graham County are federal highways.
  III. Some of the roads from Plainville lead to Nicodemus.
  IV. Some of the roads running from Hill City lead to Strong City.

CONCLUSION: Some of the roads from Plainville are county roads.
  A. The conclusion is proved by statements I-IV;
  B. The conclusion is disproved by statements I-IV.
  C. The facts are not sufficient to prove or disprove the conclusion.

KEY (CORRECT ANSWERS)

1.	A		11.	A
2.	A		12.	D
3.	A		13.	E
4.	C		14.	D
5.	A		15.	B
6.	B		16.	B
7.	A		17.	C
8.	A		18.	A
9.	A		19.	B
10.	E		20.	A

21. A
22. A
23. B
24. A
25. A

SOLUTIONS TO PROBLEMS

1. **CORRECT ANSWER: A**
   Given Statement 3, we deduce that James will not be transferred to another department. By Statement 2, we can conclude that James will be promoted.

2. **CORRECT ANSWER: A**
   Since every player on the softball team wears glasses, these individuals compose some of the people who work at the bank. Although not every person who works at the bank plays softball, those bank employees who do play softball wear glasses.

3. **CORRECT ANSWER: A**
   If Henry and June go out to dinner, we conclude that it must be on Tuesday or Thursday, which are the only two days when they have childbirth classes. This implies that if it is not Tuesday or Thursday, then this couple does not go out to dinner.

4. **CORRECT ANSWER: C**
   We can only conclude that if a person plays on the field hockey team, then he or she has both bruises and scarred knees. But there are probably a great number of people who have both bruises and scarred knees but do not play on the field hockey team. The given conclusion can neither be proven or disproven.

5. **CORRECT ANSWER: A**
   From statement 1, if Jane beats Mathias, then Lance will beat Jane. Using statement 2, we can then conclude that Christine will not win her match against Jane.

6. **CORRECT ANSWER: B**
   Statement 1 tells us that no green light can be an indicator of the belt drive status. Thus, the given conclusion must be false.

7. **CORRECT ANSWER: A**
   We already know that Ben and Elliot are in the 7th grade. Even though Hannah and Carl are in the same grade, it cannot be the 7th grade because we would then have at least four students in this 7th grade. This would contradict the third statement, which states that either two or three students are in each grade. Since Amy, Dan, and Francine are in different grade, exactly one of them must be in the 7th grade. Thus, Ben, Elliot, and exactly one of Amy, Dan, and Francine are the three students in the 7th grade.

8. **CORRECT ANSWER: A**
   One man is a teacher, who is Russian. We know that the writer is female and is Russian. Since her husband is an engineer, he cannot be the Russian teacher. Thus, her husband is of German descent, namely Mr. Stern. This means that Mr. Stern's wife is the writer. Note that one couple consists of a male Russian teacher and a female German lawyer. The other couple consists of a male German engineer and a female Russian writer.

9. **CORRECT ANSWER: A**
Since John is more than 10 inches taller than Lisa, his height is at least 46 inches. Also, John is shorter than Henry, so Henry's height must be greater than 46 inches. Thus, Lisa is the only one whose height is less than 36 inches. Therefore, she is the only one who is not allowed on the flume ride.

18. **CORRECT ANSWER: A**
Dan jumped higher than Carl, who jumped higher than Ignacio, who jumped higher than Frank. Since Martha jumped higher than Frank, every person jumped higher than Frank. Thus, Frank finished last.

19. **CORRECT ANSWER: B**
If the light is red, then the door is locked. If the door is locked, then the mill is operating. Reversing the logical sequence of these statements, if the mill is not operating, then the door is not locked, which means that the light is blue. Thus, the given conclusion is disproved.

20. **CORRECT ANSWER: A**
Using the contrapositive of statement III, Ziegfried was given his ten additional minutes, then Kimba did not learn how to shoot a basketball. Since statement IV is factual, the conclusion is proved.

21. **CORRECT ANSWER: A**
From Statements IV and I, we conclude that Sara doesn't divorce Stan. Then statement III reveals that Irene will be disappointed. Thus, the conclusion is proved.

22. **CORRECT ANSWER: A**
Statement II can be rewritten as "Delia is promoted to district manager or she misses her sales quota." Furthermore, this statement is equivalent to "If Delia makes her sales quota, then she is promoted to district manager." From statement I, we conclude that Claudia is promoted to team leader. Finally, by statement III, Thomas is promoted to assistant team leader.

23. **CORRECT ANSWER: B**
By statement IV, Clone E is not identical to any clones identical to Clone B. Statement I tells us that Clones B and D are identical. Therefore, Clone E cannot be identical to Clone D. The conclusion is disproved.

24. **CORRECT ANSWER: A**
Based on all four statements, CyberGraphics is somewhere below MainEvent. Gasco is one floor below CyberGraphics. EZ Tax is two floors below Gasco. Treehorn Audio is one floor below EZ Tax. MainEvent is four floors below Treehorn Audio. Thus, EZ Tax is two floors below Gasco and five floors above MainEvent. The conclusion is proved.

25. **CORRECT ANSWER: A**
From statement III, we know that some of the roads from Plainville lead to Nicodemus. But statement I tells us that only county roads lead to Nicodemus. Therefore, some of the roads from Plainville must be county roads. The conclusion is proved.

TEST 2

DIRECTIONS: Each question or incomplete statement is followed by several suggested answers or completions. Select the one that BEST answers the question or completes the statement. *PRINT THE LETTER OF THE CORRECT ANSWER IN THE SPACE AT THE RIGHT.*

Questions 1-9.

DIRECTIONS: In Questions 1 through 9, you will read a set of facts and a conclusion drawn from them. The conclusion may be valid or invalid, based on the facts—it's your task to determine the validity of the conclusion.

For each question, select the letter before the statement that BEST expresses the relationship between the given facts and the conclusion that has been drawn from them. Your choices are:
    A. The facts prove the conclusion;
    B. The facts disprove the conclusion; or
    C. The facts neither prove nor disprove the conclusion.

1. FACTS: Some employees in the testing department are statisticians. Most of the statisticians who work in the testing department are projection specialists. Tom Wilks works in the testing department.

    CONCLUSION: Tom Wilks is a statistician.
        A. The facts prove the conclusion.
        B. The facts disprove the conclusion.
        C. The facts neither prove nor disprove the conclusion.

2. FACTS: Ten coins are split among Hank, Lawrence, and Gail. If Lawrence gives his coins to Hank, then Hank will have more coins than Gail. If Gail gives her coins to Lawrence, then Lawrence will have more coins than Hank.

    CONCLUSION: Hank has six coins.
        A. The facts prove the conclusion.
        B. The facts disprove the conclusion.
        C. The facts neither prove nor disprove the conclusion.

3. FACTS: Nobody loves everybody. Janet loves Ken. Ken loves everybody who loves Janet.

    CONCLUSION: Everybody loves Janet.
        A. The facts prove the conclusion.
        B. The facts disprove the conclusion.
        C. The facts neither prove nor disprove the conclusion.

4. FACTS: Most of the Torres family lives in East Los Angeles. Many people in East Los Angeles celebrate Cinco de Mayo. Joe is a member of the Torres family.

   CONCLUSION: Joe lives in East Los Angeles.
   A. The facts prove the conclusion.
   B. The facts disprove the conclusion.
   C. The facts neither prove nor disprove the conclusion.

5. FACTS: Five professionals each occupy one story of a five-story office building. Dr. Kane's office is above Dr. Assad's. Dr. Johnson's office is between Dr. Kane's and Dr. Conlon's. Dr. Steen's office is between Dr. Conlon's and Dr. Assad's. Dr. Johnson is on the fourth story.

   CONCLUSION: Dr. Kane occupies the top story.
   A. The facts prove the conclusion.
   B. The facts disprove the conclusion.
   C. The facts neither prove nor disprove the conclusion.

6. FACTS: To be eligible for membership in the Yukon Society, a person must be able to either tunnel through a snowbank while wearing only a T-shirt and short, or hold his breath for two minutes under water that is 50°F. Ray can only hold his breath for a minute and a half.

   CONCLUSION: Ray can still become a member of the Yukon Society by tunneling through a snowbank while wearing a T-shirt and shorts.
   A. The facts prove the conclusion.
   B. The facts disprove the conclusion.
   C. The facts neither prove nor disprove the conclusion.

7. FACTS: A mark is worth five plunks. You can exchange four sharps for a tinplot. It takes eight marks to buy a sharp.

   CONCLUSION: A sharp is the most valuable.
   A. The facts prove the conclusion.
   B. The facts disprove the conclusion.
   C. The facts neither prove nor disprove the conclusion.

8. FACTS: There are gibbons, as well as lemurs, who like to play in the trees at the monkey house. All those who like to play in the trees at the monkey house are fed lettuce and bananas.

   CONCLUSION: Lemurs and gibbons are types of monkeys.
   A. The facts prove the conclusion.
   B. The facts disprove the conclusion.
   C. The facts neither prove nor disprove the conclusion.

9. FACTS: None of the Blackfoot tribes is a Salishan Indian tribe. Salishan Indians came from the northern Pacific Coast. All Salishan Indians live each of the Continental Divide.

   9._____

   CONCLUSION: No Blackfoot tribes live east of the Continental Divide.
   A. The facts prove the conclusion.
   B. The facts disprove the conclusion.
   C. The facts neither prove nor disprove the conclusion.

Questions 10-17.

DIRECTIONS: Questions 10 through 17 are based on the following reading passage. It is not your knowledge of the particular topic that is being tested, but your ability to reason based on what you have read. The passage is likely to detail several proposed courses of action and factors affecting these proposals. The reading passage is followed by a conclusion or outcome based on the facts in the passage, or a description of a decision taken regarding the situation. The conclusion is followed by a number of statements that have a possible connection to the conclusion. For each statement, you are to determine whether:
   A. The statement proves the conclusion.
   B. The statement supports the conclusion but does not prove it.
   C. The statement disproves the conclusion.
   D. The statement weakens the conclusion but does not disprove it.
   E. The statement has no relevance to the conclusion.

Remember that the conclusion after the passage is to be accepted as the outcome of what actually happened, and that you are being asked to evaluate the impact each statement would have had on the conclusion.

PASSAGE:

On August 12, Beverly Willey reported that she was in the elevator late on the previous evening after leaving her office on the 16th floor of a large office building. In her report, she states that a man got on the elevator at the 11th floor, pulled her off the elevator, assaulted her, and stole her purse. Ms. Willey reported that she had seen the man in the elevators and hallways of the building before. She believes that the man works in the building. Her description of him is as follows: he is tall, unshaven, with wavy brown hair and a scar on his left cheek. He walks with a pronounced limp, often dragging his left foot behind his right.

CONCLUSION: After Beverly Willey makes her report, the police arrest a 43-year-old man, Barton Black, and charge him with her assault.

10. Barton Black is a former Marine who served in Vietnam, where he sustained shrapnel wounds to the left side of his face and suffered nerve damage in his left leg.
    A. The statement proves the conclusion.
    B. The statement supports the conclusion but does not prove it.
    C. The statement disproves the conclusion.
    D. The statement weakens the conclusion but does not disprove it.
    E. The statement has no relevance to the conclusion.

10.____

11. When they arrived at his residence to question him, detectives were greeted at the door by Barton Black, who was tall and clean-shaven.
    A. The statement proves the conclusion.
    B. The statement supports the conclusion but does not prove it.
    C. The statement disproves the conclusion.
    D. The statement weakens the conclusion but does not disprove it.
    E. The statement has no relevance to the conclusion.

11.____

12. Barton Black was booked into the county jail several days after Beverly Willey's assault.
    A. The statement proves the conclusion.
    B. The statement supports the conclusion but does not prove it.
    C. The statement disproves the conclusion.
    D. The statement weakens the conclusion but does not disprove it.
    E. The statement has no relevance to the conclusion.

12.____

13. Upon further investigation, detectives discover that Beverly Willey does not work at the office building.
    A. The statement proves the conclusion.
    B. The statement supports the conclusion but does not prove it.
    C. The statement disproves the conclusion.
    D. The statement weakens the conclusion but does not disprove it.
    E. The statement has no relevance to the conclusion.

13.____

14. Upon further investigation, detectives discover that Barton Black does not work at the office building.
    A. The statement proves the conclusion.
    B. The statement supports the conclusion but does not prove it.
    C. The statement disproves the conclusion.
    D. The statement weakens the conclusion but does not disprove it.
    E. The statement has no relevance to the conclusion.

14.____

15. In the spring of the following year, Barton Black is convicted of assaulting Beverly Willey on August 11.
    A. The statement proves the conclusion.
    B. The statement supports the conclusion but does not prove it.
    C. The statement disproves the conclusion.
    D. The statement weakens the conclusion but does not disprove it.
    E. The statement has no relevance to the conclusion.

15.____

5 (#2)

16. During their investigation of the assault, detectives determine that Beverly Willey   16.____
    was assaulted on the 12th floor of the office building.
    A. The statement proves the conclusion.
    B. The statement supports the conclusion but does not prove it.
    C. The statement disproves the conclusion.
    D. The statement weakens the conclusion but does not disprove it.
    E. The statement has no relevance to the conclusion.

17. The day after Beverly Willey's assault, Barton Black fled the area and was never   17.____
    seen again.
    A. The statement proves the conclusion.
    B. The statement supports the conclusion but does not prove it.
    C. The statement disproves the conclusion.
    D. The statement weakens the conclusion but does not disprove it.
    E. The statement has no relevance to the conclusion.

Questions 18-25.

DIRECTIONS: Questions 18 through 25 each provide four factual statements and a conclusion
             based on these statements. After reading the entire question, you will decide
             whether:
             A. The conclusion is proved by statements I-IV;
             B. The conclusion is disproved by statements I-IV.
             C. The facts are not sufficient to prove or disprove the conclusion.

18. FACTUAL STATEMENTS: 18.____
    I. Among five spice jars on the shelf, the sage is to the right of the parsley.
    II. The pepper is to the left of the basil.
    III. The nutmeg is between the sage and the pepper.
    IV. The pepper is the second spice from the left.

    CONCLUSION: The safe is the farthest to the right.
    A. The conclusion is proved by statements I-IV;
    B. The conclusion is disproved by statements I-IV.
    C. The facts are not sufficient to prove or disprove the conclusion.

19. FACTUAL STATEMENTS: 19.____
    I. Gear X rotates in a clockwise direction if Switch C is in the OFF position.
    II. Gear X will rotate in a counter-clockwise direction is Switch C is ON.
    III. If Gear X is rotating in a clockwise direction, then Gear Y will not be rotating
         at all.
    IV. Switch C is ON.

    CONCLUSION: Gear X is rotating in a counter-clockwise direction.
    A. The conclusion is proved by statements I-IV;
    B. The conclusion is disproved by statements I-IV.
    C. The facts are not sufficient to prove or disprove the conclusion.

6 (#2)

20. FACTUAL STATEMENTS:
    I. Lane will leave for the Toronto meeting today only if Terence, Rourke, and Jackson all file their marketing reports by the end of the work day.
    II. Rourke will file her report on time only if Ganz submits last quarter's data.
    III. If Terence attends the security meeting, he will attend it with Jackson, and they will not file their marketing reports by the end of the work day.

    CONCLUSION: Lane will leave for the Toronto meeting today.
    A. The conclusion is proved by statements I-IV;
    B. The conclusion is disproved by statements I-IV.
    C. The facts are not sufficient to prove or disprove the conclusion.

    20.____

21. FACTUAL STATEMENTS:
    I. Bob is in second place in the Boston Marathon.
    II. Gregory is winning the Boston Marathon.
    III. There are four miles to go in the race, and Bob is gaining on Gregory at the rate of 100 yards every minute.
    IV. There are 1760 yards in a mile and Gregory's usual pace during the Boston Marathon is one mile every six minutes.

    CONCLUSION: Bob wins the Boston Marathon.
    A. The conclusion is proved by statements I-IV;
    B. The conclusion is disproved by statements I-IV.
    C. The facts are not sufficient to prove or disprove the conclusion.

    21.____

22. FACTUAL STATEMENTS:
    I. Four brothers are named Earl, John, Gary, and Pete.
    II. Earl and Pete are unmarried.
    III. John is shorter than the youngest of the four.
    IV. The oldest brother is married, and is also the tallest.

    CONCLUSION: Gary is the oldest brother.
    A. The conclusion is proved by statements I-IV;
    B. The conclusion is disproved by statements I-IV.
    C. The facts are not sufficient to prove or disprove the conclusion.

    22.____

23. FACTUAL STATEMENTS:
    I. Brigade X is ten miles from the demilitarized zone.
    II. If General Woundwort gives the order, Brigade X will advance to the demilitarized zone, but not quickly enough to reach the zone before the conflict begins.
    III. Brigade Y, five miles behind Brigade X, will not advance unless General Woundwort gives the order.
    IV. Brigade Y advances.

    23.____

CONCLUSION: Brigade X reaches the demilitarized zone before the conflict begins.
   A. The conclusion is proved by statements I-IV;
   B. The conclusion is disproved by statements I-IV.
   C. The facts are not sufficient to prove or disprove the conclusion.

24. FACTUAL STATEMENTS:
   I. Jerry has decided to take a cab from Fullerton to Elverton.
   II. Chubby Cab charges $5 plus $3 a mile.
   III. Orange Cab charges $7.50 but gives free mileage for the first 5 miles.
   IV. After the first 5 miles, Orange Cab charges $2.50 a mile.

   CONCLUSION: Orange Cab is the cheaper fare from Fullerton to Elverton.
   A. The conclusion is proved by statements I-IV;
   B. The conclusion is disproved by statements I-IV.
   C. The facts are not sufficient to prove or disprove the conclusion.

25. FACTUAL STATEMENTS:
   I. Dan is never in class when his friend Lucy is absent.
   II. Lucy is never absent unless her mother is sick.
   III. If Lucy is in class, Sergio is in class also.
   IV. Sergio is never in class when Dalton is absent.

   CONCLUSION: If Lucy is absent, Dalton may be in class.
   A. The conclusion is proved by statements I-IV;
   B. The conclusion is disproved by statements I-IV.
   C. The facts are not sufficient to prove or disprove the conclusion.

KEY (CORRECT ANSWERS)

1.	C		11.	E
2.	B		12.	B
3.	B		13.	D
4.	C		14.	E
5.	A		15.	A
6.	A		16.	E
7.	B		17.	C
8.	C		18.	B
9.	C		19.	A
10.	B		20.	C

21.	C
22.	A
23.	B
24.	A
25.	B

SOLUTIONS TO PROBLEMS

1. **CORRECT ANSWER: C**
   Statement 1 only tells us that some employees who work in the Testing Department are statisticians. This means that we need to allow the possibility that at least one person in this department is not a statistician. Thus, if a person works in the Testing Department, we cannot conclude whether or not this individual is a statistician.

2. **CORRECT ANSWER: B**
   If Hank had six coins, then the total of Gail's collection and Lawrence's collection would be four. Thus, if Gail gave all her coins to Lawrence, Lawrence would only have four coins. Thus, it would be impossible for Lawrence to have more coins than Hank.

3. **CORRECT ANSWER: B**
   Statement 1 tells us that nobody loves everybody. If everybody loved Janet, then Statement 3 would imply that Ken loves everybody. This would contradict statement 1. The conclusion is disproved.

4. **CORRECT ANSWER: C**
   Although most of the Torres family lives in East Los Angeles, we can assume that some members of this family do not live in East Los Angeles. Thus, we cannot prove or disprove that Joe, who is a member of the Torres family, lives in East Los Angeles.

5. **CORRECT ANSWER: A**
   Since Dr. Johnson is on the 4th floor, either (a) Dr. Kane is on the 5th floor and Dr. Conlon is on the 3rd floor, or (b) Dr. Kane is on the 3rd floor and Dr. Conlon is on the 5th floor. If option (b) were correct, then since Dr. Assad would be on the 1st floor, it would be impossible for Dr. Steen's office to be between Dr. Conlon and Dr. Assad's office. Therefore, Dr. Kane's office must be on the 5th floor. The order of the doctors' offices, from 5th floor down to the 1st floor is: Dr. Kane, Dr. Johnson, Dr. Conlon, Dr. Steen, Dr. Assad.

6. **CORRECT ANSWER: A**
   Ray does not satisfy the requirement of holding his breath for two minutes under water, since he can only hold is breath for one minute in that setting. But if he tunnels through a snowbank with just a T-shirt and shorts, he will satisfy the eligibility requirement. Note that the eligibility requirement contains the key word "or." So only one of the two clauses separated by "or" need to be fulfilled.

7. **CORRECT ANSWER: B**
   Statement 2 says that four sharps is equivalent to one tinplot. This means that a tinplot is worth more than a sharp. The conclusion is disproved. We note that the order of these items, from most valuable to least valuable are: tinplot, sharp, mark, plunk.

8. **CORRECT ANSWER: C**
   We can only conclude that gibbons and lemurs are fed lettuce and bananas. We can neither prove nor disprove that these animals are types of monkeys.

9. CORRECT ANSWER: C
We know that all Salishan Indians live east of the Continental Divide. But some non-members of this tribe of Indians may also live east of the Continental Divide. Since none of the members of the Blackfoot tribe belong to the Salishan Indian tribe, we cannot draw any conclusion about the location of the Blackfoot tribe with respect to the Continental Divide.

18. CORRECT ANSWER: B
Since the pepper is second from the left and the nutmeg is between the sage and the pepper, the positions 2, 3, and 4 (from the left) are pepper, nutmeg, sage. By statement II, the basil must be in position 5, which implies that the parsley is in position 1. Therefore, the basil, not the sage, is farthest to the right. The conclusion disproved.

19. CORRECT ANSWER: A
Statement II assures us that if switch C is ON, then Gear X is rotating in a counterclockwise direction. The conclusion is proved.

20. CORRECT ANSWER: C
Based on Statement IV, followed by Statement II, we conclude that Ganz and Rourke will file their reports on time. Statement III reveals that if Terence and Jackson attend the security meeting, they will fail to file their reports on time. We have no further information if Terence and Jackson attended the security meeting, so we are not able to either confirm or deny that their reports were filed on time. This implies that we cannot know for certain that Lane will leave for his meeting in Toronto.

21. CORRECT ANSWER: C
Although Bob is in second place behind Gregory, we cannot deduce how far behind Gregory he is running. At Gregory's current pace, he will cover four miles in 24 minutes. If Bob were only 100 yards behind Gregory, he would catch up to Gregory in one minute. But if Bob were very far behind Gregory, for example 5 miles, this is the equivalent of (5)(1760) = 8800 yards. Then Bob would need 8800/100 = 88 minutes to catch up to Gregory. Thus, the given facts are not sufficient to draw a conclusion.

22. CORRECT ANSWER: A
Statement II tells us that neither Earl nor Pete could be the oldest; also, either John or Gary is married. Statement IV reveals that the oldest brother is both married and the tallest. By Statement III, John cannot be the tallest. Since John is not the tallest, he is not the oldest. Thus, the oldest brother must be Gary. The conclusion is proved.

23. CORRECT ANSWER: B
By Statements III and IV, General Woundwort must have given the order to advance. Statement II then tells us that Brigade X will advance to the demilitarized zone, but not soon enough before the conflict begins. Thus, the conclusion is disproved.

11 (#2)

24. CORRECT ANSWER: A
If the distance is 5 miles or less, then the cost for the Orange Cab is only $7.50, whereas the cost for the Chubby Cab is $5 + 3x$, where x represents the number of miles traveled. For 1 to 5 miles, the cost of the Chubby Cab is between $8 and $20. This means that for a distance of 5 miles, the Orange Cab costs $7.50, whereas the Chubby Cab costs $20. After 5 miles, the cost per mile of the Chubby Cab exceeds the cost per mile of the Orange Cab. Thus, regardless of the actual distance between Fullerton and Elverton, the cost for the Orange Cab will be cheaper than that of the Chubby Cab.

25. CORRECT ANSWER: B
It looks like "Dalton" should be replaced by "Dan" in the conclusion. Then by statement I, if Lucy is absent, Dan is never in class. Thus, the conclusion is disproved.

EXAMINATION SECTION
TEST 1

DIRECTIONS: Each question or incomplete statement is followed by several suggested answers or completions. Select the one that BEST answers the question or completes the statement. *PRINT THE LETTER OF THE CORRECT ANSWER IN THE SPACE AT THE RIGHT.*

1. It is generally accepted that, of the following, the MOST important medium for developing integration and continuity in learning on the job is
   A. day-to-day experience on the job   B. the supervisory conference
   C. the staff meeting   D. the professional seminar

   1.____

2. Assume that you find that one of your workers is over-identifying with a particular client.
   Of the following, the MOST appropriate step for you to take FIRST in dealing with this situation is to
   A. transfer the cases to another worker
   B. inform the worker that he cannot give satisfactory service if he over-identifies with a client
   C. interview the client yourself to determine his feelings about his relationship with the worker
   D. arrange a conference with the worker to discuss the reasons for her over-identification with this client

   2.____

3. The one of the following which is the MOST likely reason why a newly-appointed supervisor would have a tendency to interfere actively in a relationship between one of his workers and a client is that the supervisor
   A. has unresolved feelings about relinquishing the role of worker, and has not yet accepted his role as supervisor
   B. must give direct assistance in the situation because the worker cannot handle it
   C. is attempting to share with his worker the knowledge and skill which he has developed in direct practice
   D. has not realized that immediate responsibility for work with clients has been delegated to others

   3.____

4. A worker who has a tendency to resist authority and supervision can be helped MOST effectively if, of the following, the supervisor
   A. behaves in a strict and impersonal manner so that the worker will accept his authority as a supervisor
   B. modifies the relationship so that he will be less authoritarian and threatening to the worker
   C. gives the worker a simple, matter-of-fact interpretation of the supervisory relationship and has an understanding acceptance of the worker's response
   D. temporarily establishes a peer relationship with the worker in order to overcome his resistance

   4.____

5. Before interviewing a newly-appointed worker for the first time, of the following, it is DESIRABLE for the supervisor to
   A. learn as much as he can about the worker's background and interests in order to eliminate the routine of asking questions and eliciting answers
   B. review the job information to be covered in order to make it easier to be impersonal and keep to the business at hand
   C. send the worker orientation material about the agency and the job and ask him to study it before the interview
   D. review available information about the worker in order to find an area of shared experience to serve as a *taking off* point for getting acquainted

6. In interviewing a new worker, of the following, it is IMPORTANT for the supervisor to
   A. give direction to the progress of the interview and maintain a leadership role throughout
   B. allow the worker to take the initiative in order to give him full scope for freedom of expression
   C. maintain a non-directional approach so that the worker will reveal his true attitudes and feelings
   D. avoid interrupting the worker, even though he seems to want to do all the talking

7. When a new worker, during his first few days, shows such symptoms of insecurity as *stage fright*, helpless immobility, or extreme talkativeness, of the following, it would be MOST helpful for the supervisor to
   A. start the worker out on some activity in which he is relatively secure
   B. ignore the symptoms and allow the worker to *sink or swim* on his own
   C. have a conference with the worker and interpret to him the reasons for his feelings of insecurity
   D. consider the probability that this worker may not be suited for a profession which requires skill in interpersonal relationships

8. Of the following, the MOST desirable method of minimizing workers' dependence on the supervisor and encouraging self-dependence is to
   A. hold group instead of individual supervisory conferences at regular intervals
   B. schedule individual supervisory conferences only in response to the workers' obvious need for guidance
   C. plan for progressive exposure to other opportunities for learning afforded by the agency and the community
   D. allow workers to learn by trial and error rather than by direct supervisory guidance

9. Of the following, it would NOT be appropriate for the supervisor to use early supervisory conferences with the new workers as a means of
   A. giving him direct practical help in order to get going on the job
   B. estimating the level of his native abilities, professional skills and experience
   C. getting clues as to his characteristic ways of learning in a new situation
   D. assessing his potential for future supervisory responsibility

10. Without careful planning by the supervisor for orientation of the new worker, an informal system of orientation by co-workers inevitably develops.
    Such an informal system of orientation is USUALLY
    A. *beneficial*, because many new workers learn more readily when instructed by their peers
    B. *harmful*, because informal orientation by an undesignated co-worker can lead a new worker astray instead of helping him
    C. *beneficial*, because assumption by subordinates of responsibility for orientation will free the supervisor for other urgent work
    D. *harmful*, because such informal orientation by a co-worker will tend to destroy the authority of the supervisor

11. Of the following, the BEST way for a supervisor to assist a subordinate who has unusual work pressures is to
    A. relieve him of some of his cases until the pressures subside
    B. help him to decide which cases should be given the most attention during the period of pressure, and how to provide coverage for less urgent cases
    C. inform him that he must learn to tolerate and adjust to such pressures
    D. point out that he should learn to understand the causes of the pressures, which probably resulted from his own deficiencies

12. Many supervisors have a tendency to use case records mainly for the purpose of analysis of the workers' skill or evaluation of their performance.
    Of the following, a PROBABLE result of this practice is that
    A. workers are likely to tie-in recording with supervisory evaluation of their work, without giving proper emphasis to their importance in improving service to clients
    B. the worker is likely to devote an inordinate amount of time to case records at the expense of his clients
    C. the records are likely to be too lengthy and detailed, limiting their value for other important purposes
    D. the records are likely to be of little value for administrative and research purposes

13. A common obstacle to adequate recording in a large social work agency is the fact that many workers consider recording to be a time-consuming chore.
    In order to obtain the cooperation of staff in keeping proper records, of the following, it is MOST important for an agency to provide
    A. indisputable evidence of the intelligent use of records as tools in formulating policy and improving service
    B. a system of checks and controls to assure that workers are preparing adequate and timely records
    C. adequate clerical services and mechanical equipment for recording
    D. sufficient time for recording in the organization of every job

14. The one of the following which is NOT a purpose of keeping case records in an agency is
    A. planning B. research
    C. training D. job classification

4 (#1)

15. When a supervisor is reviewing the records of a worker, of the following, he should plan to read
    A. records of new cases only, following up each interview selectively
    B. the total caseload, in order to determine which aspects of the worker's performance should be examined
    C. those records which the worker has brought to the supervisor's attention because of the need for help
    D. a block of records selected according to the worker's need for help, and some records selected at random

16. The one of the following which is the PRIMARY purpose of the regular staff meeting in an agency is
    A. initiation of action in order to get the agency's work done
    B. staff training and development
    C. program and policy determination
    D. communication of new policies and procedures

17. Of the following, group supervision in an agency is intended as a means of
    A. strengthening the total supervisory process
    B. shifting the focus of supervision from the individual to the group
    C. saving costs in terms of time and manpower
    D. influencing policy through group interaction

18. The supervisor's job brings him closer to such limiting factors in the operation of an agency as faulty administrative structure, shortage of funds and lack of facilities, inadequacies in personnel practices, community pressures, and excessive workload.
    For the supervisor to make a practice of communicating to his subordinates his feelings of frustration about such limitations in the work setting would be
    A. *appropriate*, because the worker will be more understanding of the supervisor's burdens and frustrations
    B. *inappropriate*, because the climate created will block rather than further the purposes of supervision
    C. *appropriate*, because such communication will create a more democratic climate between the worker and the supervisor
    D. *inappropriate*, because the supervisor must support and condone agency policies and practices in the presence of subordinates

19. A suggestion has been made that the teaching and administrative functions of supervision should be separated, so that the supervisor responsible for teaching would not be responsible for evaluation of the same workers.
    The one of the following which is the MOST important reason for this point of view is that
    A. elements that confer on the supervisor a position of authority and power unduly threaten the learning situation
    B. teaching skill and administrative ability do not usually go together

C. a supervisor who has been responsible for training a worker is likely to be prejudiced in his favor
D. performance evaluation and total job accountability should be two separate functions

20. In reviewing a worker's cases in preparation for a periodic evaluation, you note that she has done a uniformly good job with certain types of cases and poor work with other types of cases.
Of the following, the BEST approach for you to take in this situation is to
    A. bring this to the worker's attention, find out why she favors certain types of clients, and discuss ways in which she can improve her service to all clients
    B. bring this to the worker's attention and suggest that she may need professional counseling, as she seems to be blocked in working with certain types of cases
    C. assign to her mainly those cases which she handles best and transfer the types of cases which she handles poorly to another worker
    D. accept the fact that a worker cannot be expected to give uniformly good service to all clients, and take no further action

KEY (CORRECT ANSWERS)

1.	B	11.	B
2.	D	12.	A
3.	A	13.	A
4.	C	14.	D
5.	D	15.	D
6.	A	16.	A
7.	A	17.	A
8.	C	18.	B
9.	D	19.	A
10.	B	20.	A

TEST 2

DIRECTIONS: Each question or incomplete statement is followed by several suggested answers or completions. Select the one that BEST answers the question or completes the statement. *PRINT THE LETTER OF THE CORRECT ANSWER IN THE SPACE AT THE RIGHT.*

1. Of the following, the choice of method to be used in the supervisory process should be influenced MOST by the
   A. number and type of cases carried by each worker
   B. emotional maturity of the worker
   C. number of workers supervised and their past experience
   D. subject matter to be learned and the long-range goals of supervision

    1.____

2. In an evaluation conference with a worker, the BEST approach for the supervisor to take is to
   A. help the worker to identify his strengths as a basis for working on his weaknesses
   B. identify the worker's weaknesses and help him overcome them
   C. allow the worker to identify his weaknesses first and then suggest ways of overcoming them
   D. discuss the worker's weaknesses but emphasize his strengths

    2.____

3. Assume that a worker is discouraged about the progress of his work and feels that it is futile to attempt to cope with many of his cases.
   Of the following, it would be BEST for the supervisor to
   A. suggest to the worker that such feelings are inappropriate for a professional worker
   B. tell the worker that he must seek professional help in order to overcome these feelings
   C. reduce the worker's caseload and give him cases that are less complex
   D. review with the worker several of his cases in which there were obvious accomplishments

    3.____

4. The supervisor is responsible for providing the worker with the following means of support, with the EXCEPTION of
   A. interest and advice on his personal problems
   B. instruction on community resources
   C. inspiration for carrying out the work of the agency
   D. understanding his strengths and limitations

    4.____

5. When a worker frequently takes the initiative in asking questions and discussing problems during a supervisory conference, this is PROBABLY an indication that the
   A. supervisor is not sufficiently interested in the work
   B. conference is a positive learning experience for the worker
   C. worker is hostile and resists supervision
   D. supervisor's position of authority is in question

    5.____

6. When a supervisor finds that one of his workers cannot accept criticism, of the following, it would be BEST for the supervisor to
    A. have the worker transferred to another supervisor
    B. warn the worker of disciplinary proceedings unless his attitude changes
    C. have the worker suspended after explaining the reason
    D. explore with the worker his attitude toward authority

7. Of the following, the condition which the inexperienced worker is LEAST likely to be aware of, without the guidance of the supervisor, is
    A. when he is successful in helping a client
    B. when he is not making progress in helping a client
    C. that he has a personal bias toward certain clients
    D. that he feels insecure because of lack of experience

8. The supervisor should provide an inexperienced worker with controls as well as freedom MAINLY because controls will
    A. enable him to set up his own controls sooner
    B. put him in a situation which is closer to the realities of life
    C. help him to use authority in handling a casework problem
    D. give him a feeling of security and lay the foundation for future self-direction

9. A result of the use of summarized case recording by the worker is that it
    A. gives the supervisor more responsibility for selecting cases to discuss in conference
    B. makes more time available for other activities
    C. lowers the morale of many workers
    D. decreases discussion of cases by the worker and the supervisor

10. The distinction between the role of professional workers and the role of auxiliary or sub-professional workers in an agency is based upon the
    A. position within the agency hierarchy
    B. amount of close supervision given
    C. emergent nature of tasks assigned
    D. functions performed

11. Of the following, the MOST important source of learning for the worker should be
    A. departmental directives and professional literature
    B. his co-workers in the agency
    C. the content of in-service training courses
    D. the clients in his caseload

12. A client is MOST likely to feel that he is receiving acceptance and understanding if the social worker
    A. gets detailed information about the client's problem
    B. demonstrates that he realistically understands the client's problem
    C. has an intellectual understanding of the client's problem
    D. offers the client assurance of assistance

13. A client will be MORE encouraged to speak freely about his problems if the worker
    A. avoids asking too many questions
    B. asks leading rather than pointed questions
    C. suggests possible answers
    D. identifies with the client

14. A client would be MOST likely to be able to accept help in a time of crisis and need if the worker
    A. explains agency policy to him
    B. responds immediately to the client's need
    C. explains why help cannot be given immediately
    D. reaches out to help the client establish his rightful claim for assistance

15. It is a generally accepted principle that the worker should interpret for himself what the client is saying, but usually should not pass his interpretation on to the client because the client
    A. will become hostile to the worker
    B. should arrive at his own conclusions at his own pace
    C. must request the interpretation first
    D. usually wants facts, rather than the worker's interpretation

16. In evaluating the client's capacity to cope with his problems, it is MOST important for the worker to assess his ability to
    A. form close relationships   B. ask for help
    C. express his hostility   D. verbalize his difficulties

17. When a worker finds that he disagrees strongly with an agency policy, it is DESIRABLE for him to
    A. share his feelings about the policy with his client
    B. understand fully why he has such strong feelings about the policy
    C. refer cases involving the policy to his supervisor
    D. refuse to give help in cases involving the policy

18. Which of the following practices is BEST for a supervisor to use when assigning work to his staff?
    A. Give workers with seniority the most difficult jobs
    B. Assign all unimportant work to the slower workers
    C. Permit each employee to pick the job he prefers
    D. Make assignments based on the workers' abilities

19. In which of the following instances is a supervisor MOST justified in giving commands to people under his supervision?
    When
    A. they delay in following instructions which have been given to them clearly
    B. they become relaxed and slow about work, and he wants to speed up their production
    C. he must direct them in an emergency situation
    D. he is instructing them on jobs that are unfamiliar to them

20. Which of the following supervisory actions or attitudes is MOST likely to result in getting subordinates to try to do as much work as possible for a supervisor?
    He
    A. shows that his most important interest is in schedules and production goals
    B. consistently pressures his staff to get the work out
    C. never fails to let them know he is in charge
    D. considers their abilities and needs while requiring that production goals be met

KEY (CORRECT ANSWERS)

1.	D	11.	D
2.	A	12.	B
3.	D	13.	D
4.	A	14.	D
5.	B	15.	B
6.	D	16.	A
7.	C	17.	B
8.	D	18.	D
9.	B	19.	C
10.	D	20.	D

TEST 3

DIRECTIONS: Each question or incomplete statement is followed by several suggested answers or completions. Select the one that BEST answers the question or completes the statement. *PRINT THE LETTER OF THE CORRECT ANSWER IN THE SPACE AT THE RIGHT.*

1. One of your workers comes to you and complains in an angry manner about your having chosen him for some particular assignment. In your opinion, the subject of the complaint is trivial land unimportant, but it seems to be quite important to your worker.
   The BEST of the following actions for you to take in this situation is to
   A. allow the worker to continue talking until he has calmed down and then explain the reasons for your having chosen him for that particular assignment
   B. warn the worker to moderate his tone of voice at once because he is bordering on insubordination
   C. tell the worker in a friendly tone that he is making a tremendous fuss over an extremely minor matter
   D. point out to the worker that you are his immediate supervisor and that you are running the unit in accordance with official policy

1.____

2. The one of the following which is the LEAST desirable action for an assistant supervisor to take in disciplining a subordinate for an infraction of the rules is to
   A. caution him against repetition of the infraction, even if it is minor
   B. point out his progress in applying the rules at the same time that you reprimand him
   C. be as specific as possible in reprimanding him for rule infractions
   D. allow a cooling-off period to elapse before reprimanding him

2.____

3. A training program for workers assigned to the intake section should include actual practice in simulated interviews under simulated conditions.
   The one of the following educational principles which is the CHIEF justification for this statement is that
   A. the workers will remember what they see better and longer than what they read or hear
   B. the workers will learn more effectively by actually doing the act themselves than they would learn from watching others do it
   C. the conduct of simulated interviews once or twice will enable them to cope with the real situation with little difficulty
   D. a training program must employ methods of a practical nature if the workers are to find anything of lasting value in it

3.____

4. In order for a supervisor to employ the system of democratic leadership in his supervision, it would generally be BEST for him to
   A. allow his subordinates to assist in deciding on methods of work performance and job assignments but only in those areas where decisions have not been made on higher administrative levels

4.____

76

B. allow his subordinates to decide how to do the required work, interposing his authority when work is not completed on schedule or is improperly completed
C. attempt to make assignments of work to individuals only of the type which they enjoy doing
D. maintain control over job assignment and work production, but allow the subordinates to select methods of work and internal conditions of work at democratically conducted staff conferences

5. In a unit in which supervision has been considered quite effective, it has become necessary to press for above-normal production for a limited period to achieve a required goal.
   The one of the following which is a LEAST likely result of this pressure is that
   A. there will be more *griping* by employees
   B. some workers will do both more and better work than has been normal for them
   C. there will be an enhanced feeling of group unity
   D. there will be increased absenteeism

6. For a supervisor to encourage competitive feelings among his staff is
   A. *advisable*, chiefly because the workers will perform more efficiently when they have proper motivation
   B. *inadvisable*, chiefly because the workers will not perform well under the pressure of competition
   C. *advisable*, chiefly because the workers will have a greater incentive to perform their job properly
   D. *inadvisable*, chiefly because the workers may focus their attention on areas where they excel and neglect other essential aspects of the job

7. In selecting jobs to be assigned to a new worker, the supervisor should assign those jobs which
   A. give the worker the greatest variety of experience
   B. offer the worker the greatest opportunity to achieve concrete results
   C. present the worker with the greatest stimulation because of their interesting nature
   D. require the least amount of contact with outside agencies

8. A supervisor should avoid a detailed discussion of a worker-client interview with a new worker before the worker has fully recorded the interview CHIEFLY because such a discussion might
   A. cover matters which are already fully covered and explained in the written record
   B. make the worker forget some important deal learned during the interview
   C. color the recording according to the worker's reaction to his supervisor's opinions
   D. minimize the worker's feeling of having reached a decision independently

9. Some supervisors encourage their worker to submit a list of their questions about specific jobs or their comments about problems they wish to discuss in advance of the worker-supervisor conference.
This practice is
   A. *desirable*, chiefly because it helps to stimulate and focus the worker's thinking about his caseload
   B. *undesirable*, chiefly because it will stifle the worker's free expression of his problems and attitudes
   C. *desirable,* chiefly because it will allow the conference to move along more smoothly and quickly
   D. *undesirable*, chiefly because it will restrict the scope of the conference and the variety of jobs discussed

9._____

10. An alert supervisor hears a worker apparently giving the wrong information to a client and immediately reprimands him severely.
For the supervisor to reprimand the worker at his point is poor CHIEFLY because
   A. instruction must precede correct performance
   B. oral reprimands are less effective than written reprimands
   C. the worker was given no opportunity to explain his reasons for what he did
   D. more effective training can be obtained by discussing the errors with a group of workers

10._____

11. The one of the following circumstances when it would generally be MOST proper for a supervisor to do a job himself rather than to train a subordinate to do the job is when it is
   A. a job which the supervisor enjoys doing and does well
   B. not a very time-consuming job but an important one
   C. difficult to train another to do the job, yet is not difficult for the supervisor to do
   D. unlikely that this or any similar job will have to be done again at any future time

11._____

12. Effective training of subordinates requires that the supervisor understand certain facts about learning and forgetting processes.
Among these is the fact that people GENERALLY
   A. forget what they learned at a much greater rate during the first day than during subsequent periods
   B. both learn and forget at a relatively constant rate and this rate is dependent upon their general intellectual capacity
   C. learn at a relatively constant rate except for periods of assimilation when the quantity of retained learning decreases while information is becoming firmly fixed in the mind
   D. learn very slowly at first when introduced to a new topic, after which there is a great increase in the rate of learning

12._____

13. It has been suggested that a subordinate who likes his superior will tend to do better work than one who does not.
    According to the MOST widely held current theories of supervision, this suggestion is a
    A. *bad* one, since personal relationships tend to interfere with proper professional relationships
    B. *bad* one, since the strongest motivating factors are fear and uncertainty
    C. *good* one, since liking one's superior is a motivating factor for good work performance
    D. *good* one, since liking one's supervisor is the most important factor in employee performance

14. One factor which might be given consideration in deciding upon the optimum span of control of a supervisor over his immediate subordinates is the position of the supervisor in the hierarchy of the organization.
    It is generally considered proper that the number of subordinates immediately supervised by a higher, upper echelon supervisor _____ the number supervised by lower level supervisors.
    A. is unrelated to and tends to form no pattern with
    B. should be about the same as
    C. should be larger than
    D. should be smaller than

15. The one of the following instances when it is MOST important for an upper level supervisor to follow the chain of command is when he is
    A. communicating decisions   B. communicating information
    C. receiving suggestions   D. seeking information

16. At the end of his probationary period, a supervisor should be considered potentially valuable in his position if he shows
    A. awareness of his areas of strength and weakness, identification with the administration of the department, and ability to learn under supervision
    B. skill in work, supervision, and administration, and a friendly democratic approach to the staff
    C. knowledge of departmental policies and procedures and ability to carry them out, ability to use authority, and ability to direct the work of the staff
    D. an identification with the department, acceptance of responsibility, and ability to give help to the individuals who are to be supervised

17. Good supervision is selective because
    A. it is not necessary to direct all the activities of the person
    B. a supervisor would never have time to know the whole caseload of a worker
    C. workers resent too much help from a supervisor
    D. too much reading is a waste of valuable time

18. An important administrative problem is how precisely to define the limits of authority that is delegated to subordinate supervisors.
Such definition of limits of authority should be
    A. as precise as possible and practicable in all areas
    B. as precise as possible and practicable in areas of function, but should allow considerable flexibility in the area of personnel management
    C. as precise as possible and practicable in the area
    D. of personnel management, but should allow considerable flexibility in the areas of function
    E. in general terms so as to allow considerable flexibility both in the areas of function and in the areas of personnel management

18.____

19. Experts in the field of personnel relations feel that it is generally a bad practice for subordinate employees to become aware of pending or contemplated changes in policy or organizational set-up via the *grapevine* CHIEFLY because
    A. evidence that one or more responsible officials have proved untrustworthy will undermine confidence in the agency
    B. the information disseminated by this method is seldom entirely accurate and generally spreads needless unrest among the subordinate staff
    C. the subordinate staff may conclude that the administration feels the staff cannot be trusted with the true information
    D. the subordinate staff may conclude that the administration lacks the courage to make an unpopular announcement through official channels

19.____

20. Supervision is subject to many interpretations, depending on the area in which it functions.
Of the following, the statement which represents the MOST appropriate meaning of supervision as it is known in social work practice is that it
    A. is a leadership process for the development of new leaders
    B. is an educational and administrative process aimed at teaching personnel the goal of improved service to the client
    C. is an activity aimed chiefly at insuring that workers will adhere to all agency directives
    D. provides the opportunity for administration to secure staff reaction to agency policies

20.____

21. A supervisor may utilize various methods in the supervisory process.
The one of the following upon which sound supervisory practice rests in the selection of supervisory techniques is
    A. an estimate of the worker arrived at through current and past evaluation of performance as well as through worker's participation
    B. the previous supervisor's evaluation and recommendation
    C. the worker's expression of his personal preference for certain types of experience
    D. the amount of time available to supervisor and supervisee

21.____

22. It is the practice of some supervisors, when they believe that it would be desirable for a subordinate to take a particular action in a case, to inform the subordinate of this in the form of a suggestion rather than in the form of a direct order.
In general, this method of getting a subordinate to take the desired action is
    A. *inadvisable*; it may create in the mind of the subordinate the impression that the supervisor is uncertain about the efficacy of her plan and is trying to avoid whatever responsibility she may have in resolving the case
    B. *advisable*; it provides the subordinate with the maximum opportunity to use her own judgment in handling the case
    C. *inadvisable*; it provides the subordinate with no clear-cut direction and, therefore, is likely to leave her with a feeling of uncertainty and frustration
    D. *advisable*; it presents the supervisor's view in a manner which will be most likely to evoke the subordinate's cooperation

23. A veteran supervisor noticed that one of her workers of average ability had begun developing some bad work habits, becoming especially careless in her recordkeeping. After reprimand from the supervisor, the investigator corrected her errors and has been doing satisfactory work since then.
For the supervisor to keep referring to this period of poor work during her weekly conferences with this employee would generally be considered poor personnel practice CHIEFLY because
    A. praise rather than criticism is generally the best method to use in improving the work of an unsatisfactory worker
    B. the supervisor cannot know whether the employee's errors will follow an established pattern
    C. the fault which evoked the original negative criticism no longer exists
    D. this would tend to frustrate the worker by making her strive overly hard to reach a level of productivity which is beyond her ability to achieve

24. Assume that you are now a supervisor in a specific unit. Two experienced investigators in your unit, both of whom do above average work, have for some time not gotten along with each other for personal reasons Their attitude toward one another has suddenly become hostile and noisy disagreement has taken place in the office.
The BEST action for you to take FIRST in this situation is to
    A. transfer one of the two investigators to another unit where contact with the other investigator will be unnecessary
    B. discuss the problem with the two investigators together, insisting that they confide in you and tell you the cause of their mutual antagonism
    C. confer with the two investigators separately, pointing out to each the need to adopt an adult professional attitude with respect to their on-the-job relations
    D. advise the two investigators that should the situation grow worse, disciplinary action will be considered

25. It has long been recognized that relationships exist between worker morale and working conditions.
The one of the following which BEST clarifies these existing relationships is that morale is
   A. affected for better or worse in direct relationship to the magnitude of the changes in working conditions for better or worse
   B. better when working conditions are better
   C. little affected by working conditions so long as the working conditions do not approach the intolerable
   D. more affected by the degree of interest shown in providing good working conditions than by the actual conditions and may, perversely, be highest when working conditions are worst

25.____

KEY (CORRECT ANSWERS)

1.	A		11.	D
2.	D		12.	A
3.	B		13.	C
4.	A		14.	D
5.	D		15.	A
6.	D		16.	D
7.	B		17.	A
8.	C		18.	A
9.	A		19.	B
10.	C		20.	B

21.	A
22.	D
23.	C
24.	C
25.	D

EXAMINATION SECTION
TEST 1

DIRECTIONS: Each question or incomplete statement is followed by several suggested answers or completions. Select the one that BEST answers the question or completes the statement. *PRINT THE LETTER OF THE CORRECT ANSWER IN THE SPACE AT THE RIGHT.*

1. Which one of the following generalizations is MOST likely to be INACCURATE and lead to judgmental errors in communication?
    A. A supervisor must be able to read with understanding.
    B. Misunderstanding may lead to dislike.
    C. Anyone can listen to another person and understand what he means.
    D. It is usually desirable to let a speaker talk until he is finished.

    1.____

2. Assume that, as a supervisor, you have been directed to inform your subordinates about the implementation of a new procedure which will affect their work.
   While communicating this information, you should do all of the following EXCEPT
    A. obtain the approval of your subordinates regarding the new procedure
    B. explain the reason for implementing the new procedure
    C. hold a staff meeting at a time convenient to most of your subordinates
    D. encourage a productive discussion of the new procedure

    2.____

3. Assume that you are in charge of a section that handles requests for information on matters received from the public. One day, you observe that a clerk under your supervision is using a method to log-in requests for information that is different from the one specified by you in the past. Upon questioning the clerk, you discover that instructions changing the old procedure were delivered orally by your supervisor on a day on which you were absent from the office.
   Of the following, the MOST appropriate action for you to take is to
    A. tell the clerk to revert to the old procedure at once
    B. ask your supervisor for information about the change
    C. call your staff together and tell them that no existing procedure is to be changed unless you direct that it be done
    D. write a memo to your supervisor suggesting that all future changes in procedure are to be in writing and that they be directed to you

    3.____

4. At the first meeting with your staff after appointment as a supervisor, you find considerable indifference and some hostility among the participants.
   Of the following, the MOST appropriate way to handle this situation is to
    A. disregard the attitudes displayed and continue to make your presentation until you have completed it
    B. discontinue your presentation but continue the meeting and attempt to find out the reasons for their attitudes

    4.____

83

C. warm up your audience with some good-natured statements and anecdotes and then proceed with your presentation
D. discontinue the meeting and set up personal interviews with the staff members to try to find out the reason for their attitude

5. In order to start the training of a new employee, it has been a standard practice to have him read a manual of instructions or procedures.
   This method is currently being replaced by the _____ method.
   A. audio-visual
   B. conference
   C. lecture
   D. programmed instruction

   5._____

6. Of the following subjects, the one that can usually be successfully taught by a first-line supervisor who is training his subordinates is:
   A. theory and philosophy of management
   B. human relations
   C. responsibilities of a supervisor
   D. job skills

   6._____

7. Assume that as supervisor you are training a clerk who is experiencing difficulty learning a new task.
   Which of the following would be the LEAST effective approach to take when trying to solve this problem? To
   A. ask questions which will reveal the clerk's understanding of the task
   B. take a different approach in explaining the task
   C. give the clerk an opportunity to ask questions about the task
   D. make sure the clerk knows you are watching his work closely

   7._____

8. One school of management and supervision involves participation by employees in the setting of group goals and in the sharing of responsibility for the operation of the unit.
   If this philosophy were applied to a unit consisting of professional and clerical personnel, one should expect
   A. the professional and clerical personnel to participate with equal effectiveness in operating areas and policy areas
   B. the professional personnel to participate with greater effectiveness than the clerical personnel in policy areas
   C. the clerical personnel to participate with greater effectiveness than the professional personnel in operating areas
   D. greater participation by clerical personnel but with less responsibility for their actions

   8._____

9. With regard to productivity, high morale among employees generally indicates a
   A. history of high productivity
   B. nearly absolute positive correlation with high productivity
   C. predisposition to be productive under facilitating leadership and circumstances
   D. complacency which has little effect on productivity

   9._____

10. Assume that you are going to organize the professionals and clerks under your supervision into work groups or team of two or three employees.
Of the following, the step which is LEAST likely to foster the successful development of each group is to
    A. allow friends to work together in the group
    B. provide special help and attention to employees with no friends in their group
    C. frequently switch employees from group to group
    D. rotate jobs within the group in order to strengthen group identification

11. Following are four statements which might be made by an employee to his supervisor during a performance evaluation interview.
Which of the statements BEST provides a basis for developing a plan to improve the employee's performance?
    A. *I understand that you are dissatisfied with my work and I will try harder in the future.*
    B. *I feel that I've been making too many careless clerical errors recently.*
    C. *I am aware that I will be subject to disciplinary action if my work does not improve within one month.*
    D. *I understand that this interview is simply a requirement of your job and not a personal attack on me.*

12. Three months ago, Mr. Smith and his supervisor, Mrs. Jones, developed a plan which was intended to correct Mr. Smith's inadequate job performance. Now, during a follow-up interview, Mr. Smith, who thought his performance had satisfactorily improved, has been informed that Mrs. Jones is still dissatisfied with his work.
Of the following, it is MOST likely that the disagreement occurred because, when formulating the plan, they did NOT
    A. set realistic goals for Mr. Smith's performance
    B. set a reasonable time limit for Mr. Smith to effect his improvement in performance
    C. provide for adequate training to improve Mr. Smith's skills
    D. establish performance standards for measuring Mr. Smith's progress

13. When a supervisor delegates authority to subordinates, there are usually many problems to overcome, such as inadequately trained subordinates and poor planning.
All of the following are means of increasing the effectiveness of delegation EXCEPT:
    A. Defining assignments in the light of results expected
    B. Maintaining open lines of communication
    C. Establishing tight controls so that subordinates will stay within the bounds of the area of delegation
    D. Providing rewards for successful assumption of authority by a subordinate

14. Assume that one of your subordinates has arrived late for work several times during the current month. The last time he was late you had warned him that another unexcused lateness would result informal disciplinary action.
If the employee arrives late for work again during this month, the FIRST action you should take is to
    A. give the employee a chance to explain this lateness
    B. give the employee a written copy of your warning
    C. tell the employee that you are recommending formal disciplinary action
    D. tell the employee that you will give him only one more chance before recommending formal disciplinary action

15. In trying to decide how many subordinates a manager can control directly, one of the determinants is how much the manager can reduce the frequency and time consumed in contacts with his subordinates.
Of the following, the factor which LEAST influences the number and direction of these contacts is:
    A. How well the manager delegates authority
    B. The rate at which the organization is changing
    C. The control techniques used by the manager
    D. Whether the activity is line or staff

16. Systematic rotation of employees through lateral transfer within a government organization to provide for managerial development is
    A. *good*, because systematic rotation develops specialists who learn to do many jobs well
    B. *bad*, because the outsider upsets the status quo of the existing organization
    C. *good*, because rotation provides challenge and organizational flexibility
    D. *bad*, because it is upsetting to employees to be transferred within a service

17. Assume that you are required to provide an evaluation of the performance of your subordinates.
Of the following factors, it is MOST important that the performance evaluation include a rating of each employee's
    A. initiative   B. productivity   C. intelligence   D. personality

18. When preparing performance evaluations of your subordinates, one way to help assure that you are rating each employee fairly is to
    A. prepare a list of all employees and all the rating factors and rate all employees on one rating factor before going on to the next factor
    B. prepare a list of all your employees and all the rating factors and rate each employee on all factors before going on to the next employee
    C. discuss all the ratings you anticipate giving with another supervisor in order to obtain an unbiased opinion
    D. discuss each employee with his co-workers in order to obtain peer judgment of worth before doing any rating

19. A managerial plan which would include the GREATEST control is a plan which is
    A. spontaneous and geared to each new job that is received
    B. detailed and covering an extended time period
    C. long-range and generalized, allowing for various interpretations
    D. specific and prepared daily

20. Assume that you are preparing a report which includes statistical data covering increases in budget allocations of four agencies for the past ten years.
    For you to represent the statistical data pictorially or graphically within the report is a
    A. *poor* idea, because you should be able to make statistical data understandable through the use of words
    B. *good* idea, because it is easier for the reader to understand pictorial representation rather than quantities of words conveying statistical data
    C. *poor* idea, because using pictorial representation in a report may make the report too expensive to print
    D. *good* idea, because a pictorial representation makes the report appear more attractive than the use of many words to convey the statistical data

KEY (CORRECT ANSWERS)

1.	C	11.	A
2.	A	12.	B
3.	B	13.	C
4.	D	14.	A
5.	D	15.	D
6.	D	16.	C
7.	D	17.	B
8.	B	18.	A
9.	C	19.	B
10.	C	20.	B

TEST 2

DIRECTIONS: Each question or incomplete statement is followed by several suggested answers or completions. Select the one that BEST answers the question or completes the statement. *PRINT THE LETTER OF THE CORRECT ANSWER IN THE SPACE AT THE RIGHT.*

1. Research studies have shown that supervisors of groups with high production records USUALLY
   A. give detailed instructions, constantly check on progress, and insist on approval of all decisions before implementation
   B. do considerable paperwork and other work similar to that performed by subordinates
   C. think of themselves as team members on the same level as others in the work group
   D. perform tasks traditionally associated with managerial functions

2. Mr. Smith, a bureau chief, is summoned by his agency's head in a conference to discuss Mr. Jones, an accountant who works in one of the divisions of his bureau. Mr. Jones has committed an error of such magnitude as to arouse the agency head's concern.
   After agreeing with the other conferees that a severe reprimand would be the appropriate punishment, Mr. Smith SHOULD
   A. arrange for Mr. Jones to explain the reasons for his error to the agency head
   B. send a memorandum to Mr. Jones, being careful that the language emphasizes the nature of the error rather than Mr. Jones' personal faults
   C. inform Mr. Jones' immediate supervisor of the conclusion reached at the conference, and let the supervisor take the necessary action
   D. suggest to the agency head that no additional action be taken against Mr. Jones because no further damage will be caused by the error

3. Assume that Ms. Thomson, a unit chief, has determined that the findings of an internal audit have been seriously distorted as a result of careless errors. The audit had been performed by a group of auditors in her unit and the errors were overlooked by the associate accountant in charge of the audit. Ms. Thomson has decided to delay discussing the matter with the associate accountant and the staff who performed the audit until she verifies certain details, which may require prolonged investigation.
   Mrs. Thomson's method of handling this situation is
   A. *appropriate*; employees should not be accused of wrongdoing until all the facts have been determined
   B. *inappropriate*; the employees involved may assume that the errors were considered unimportant
   C. *appropriate*; employees are more likely to change their behavior as a result of disciplinary action taken after a *cooling off* period
   D. *inappropriate*; the employees involved may have forgotten the details and become emotionally upset when confronted with the facts

4. After studying the financial situation in his agency, an administrative accountant decides to recommend centralization of certain accounting functions which are being performed in three different bureaus of the organization
The one of the following which is MOST likely to be a DISADVANTAE if this recommendation is implemented is that
   A. there may be less coordination of the accounting procedure because central direction is not so close to the day-to-day problems as the personnel handling them in each specialized accounting unit
   B. the higher management levels would not be able to make emergency decisions in as timely a manner as the more involved, lower-level administrators who are closer to the problem
   C. it is more difficult to focus the attention of the top management in order to resolve accounting problems because of the many other activities top management is involved in at the same time
   D. the accuracy of upward and inter-unit communication may be reduced because centralization may require insertion of more levels of administration in the chain of command

5. Of the following assumptions about the role of conflict in an organization, the one which is the MOST accurate statement of the approach of modern management theorists is that conflict
   A. can usually be avoided or controlled
   B. serves as a vital element in organizational change
   C. works against attainment of organizational goals
   D. provides a constructive outlet for problem employees

6. Which of the following is generally regarded as the BEST approach for a supervisor to follow in handling grievances brought by subordinates?
   A. Avoid becoming involved personally
   B. Involve the union representative in the first stage of discussion
   C. Settle the grievance as soon as possible
   D. Arrange for arbitration by a third party

7. Assume that supervisors of similar-sized accounting units in city, state, and federal offices were interviewed and observed at their work. It was found that the ways they acted in and viewed their roles tended to be very similar, regardless of who employed them.
Which of the following is the BEST explanation of this similarity
   A. A supervisor will ordinarily behave in conformance to his own self-image.
   B. Each role in an organization, including the supervisory role, calls for a distinct type of personality.
   C. The supervisor role reflects an exceptionally complex pattern of human response.
   D. The general nature of the duties and responsibilities of the supervisory position determines the role.

8. Which of the following is NOT consistent with the findings of recent research about the characteristics of successful top managers?
   A. They are *inner-directed* and not overly concerned with pleasing others.
   B. They are challenged by situations filled with high risk and ambiguity.
   C. They tend to stay on the same job for long periods of time.
   D. They consider it more important to handle critical assignments successfully than to do routine work well.

9. As a supervisor, you have to give subordinates operational guidelines.
   Of the following, the BEST reason for providing them with information about the overall objectives within which their operations fit is that the subordinates will
   A. be more likely to carry out the operation according to your expectations
   B. know that there is a legitimate reason for carrying out the operation in the way you have prescribed
   C. be more likely to handle unanticipated problems that may arise without having to take up your time
   D. more likely to transmit the operating instructions correctly to their subordinates

10. A supervisor holds frequent meetings with his staff.
    Of the following, the BEST approach he can take in order to elicit productive discussions at these meetings is for him to
    A. ask questions of those who attend
    B. include several levels of supervisors at the meetings
    C. hold the meetings at a specified time each week
    D. begin each meeting with a statement that discussion is welcomed

11. Of the following, the MOST important action that a supervisor can take to increase the productivity of a subordinate is to
    A. increase his uninterrupted work time
    B. increase the number of reproducing machines available in the office
    C. provide clerical assistance whenever he requests it
    D. reduce the number of his assigned tasks

12. Assume that, as a supervisor, you find out that you often must countermand or modify your original staff memos.
    If this practice continues, which one of the following situations is MOST likely to occur? The
    A. staff will not bother to read your memos
    B. office files will become cluttered
    C. staff will delay acting on your memos
    D. memos will be treated routinely

13. In making management decisions, the committee approach is often used by managers.
    Of the following, the BEST reason for using this approach is to
    A. prevent any one individual from assuming too much authority
    B. allow the manager to bring a wider range of experience and judgment to bear on the problem

C. allow the participation of all staff members, which will make them feel more committed to the decisions reached
D. permit the rapid transmission of information about decisions reached to the staff members concerned

14. In establishing standards for the measurement of the performance of a management project team, it is MOST important for the project manager to
    A. identify and define the objectives of the project
    B. determine the number of people who will be assigned to the project team
    C. evaluate the skills of the staff who will be assigned to the project team
    D. estimate fairly accurately the length of time required to complete each phase of the project

15. It is virtually impossible to tell an employee either that he is not good as another employee or that he does not measure up to a desirable level of performance, without having him feel threatened, rejected, and discouraged.
    In accordance with the foregoing observation, a supervisor who is concerned about the performance of the less efficient members of his staff should realize that
    A. he might obtain better results by not discussing the quality and quantity of their work with them, but by relying instead on the written evaluation of their performance to motivate their improvement
    B. since he is required to discuss their performance with them, he should do so in words of encouragement and in so friendly a manner as to not destroy their morale
    C. he might discuss their work in a general way, without mentioning any of the specifics about the quality of their performance, with the expectation that they would understand the full implications of his talk
    D. he should make it a point, while telling them of their poor performance, to mention that their work is as good as that of some of the other employees in the unit

16. Some advocates of management-by-objectives procedures in public agencies have been urging that this method of operations be expanded to encompass all agencies of the government, for one or more of the following reasons, not all of which may be correct:
    I. The MBO method is likely to succeed because it embraces the practice of setting near-term goals for the subordinate manager, reviewing accomplishments at an appropriate time, and repeating this process indefinitely
    II. Provision for authority to perform the tasks assigned as goals in the MBO method is normally not needed because targets are set in quantitative or qualitative terms and specific times for accomplishment are arranged in short-term, repetitive intervals
    III. Many other appraisal-of-performance programs failed because both supervisors and subordinates resisted them, while the MBO approach is not instituted until there is an organizational commitment to it
    IV. Personal accountability is clearly established through the MBO approach because verifiable results are set up in the process of formulating the targets

Which of the choices below includes ALL of the foregoing statements that are CORRECT?
A. I, III B. II, IV C. I, II, III, IV D. I, III, IV

17. In preparing an organizational structure, the PRINCIPAL guideline for locating staff units is to place them
    A. all under a common supervisor
    B. as close as possible to the activities they serve
    C. as close to the chief executive as possible without over-extending his span of control
    D. at the lowest operational level

18. The relative importance of any unit in a department can be LEAST reliably judged by the
    A. amount of office space allocated to the unit
    B. number of employees in the unit
    C. rank of the individual who heads the unit
    D. rank of the individual to whom the unit head reports directly

19. Those who favor Planning-Programming-Budgeting Systems (PPBS) as a new method of governmental financial administration emphasize that PPBS
    A. applies statistical measurements which correlate highly with criteria
    B. makes possible economic systems analysis, including an explicit examination of alternatives
    C. makes available scarce government resources which can be coordinated on a government-wide basis and shared between local units of government
    D. shifts the emphasis in budgeting methods to an automated system of data processing

20. The term applied to computer processing which processes data concurrently with a given activity and provides results soon enough to influence the selection of a course of action is _____ processing.
    A. realtime   B. batch
    C. random access   D. integrated data

KEY (CORRECT ANSWERS)

1.	D	11.	A
2.	C	12.	C
3.	B	13.	B
4.	D	14.	A
5.	B	15.	B
6.	C	16.	D
7.	D	17.	B
8.	C	18.	B
9.	C	19.	B
10.	A	20.	A

PREPARING WRITTEN MATERIAL

INTRODUCTION

These questions test for the ability to present information clearly and accurately, and to organize paragraphs logically and comprehensibly. For some questions, you will be given information in two or three sentences followed by four restatements of the information. You must then choose the best version. For other questions, you will be given paragraphs with their sentences out of order. You must then choose, from four suggestions, the BEST order for the sentences. There will be 15 questions in this subject on the written test.

Test Task: There are two separate test tasks in this subject area.

- For the first, Information Presentation, you will be given information in two or three sentences, followed by four restatements of the information. You must then choose the best version.

- For the second, Paragraph Organization, you will be given paragraphs with their sentences out of order, and then be asked to choose, from among four suggestions, the best order for the sentences. There will be five Paragraph Organization questions on the written test.

Information Presentation

1. Martin Wilson failed to take proper precautions. His failure to take proper precautions caused a personal injury accident.
   Which one of the following BEST presents the information above?
   A. Martin Wilson failed to take proper precautions that caused a personal injury accident.
   B. Proper precautions, which Martin Wilson failed to take, caused a personal injury accident.
   C. Martin Wilson's failure to take proper precautions caused a personal injury accident.
   D. Martin Wilson, who failed to take proper precautions, was in a personal injury accident.

1.____

Paragraph Organization

The following question is based upon a group of sentences. The sentences are shown out of sequence, but when correctly arranged, they form a connected, well-organize paragraph. Read the sentences, and then answer the question about the best arrangement of these sentences.

2.
I. Eventually, they piece all of this information together and make a choice.
II. Before actually deciding upon a job in nutrition services, people usually think about several possibilities.
III. They imagine themselves in different situations, and in so doing, they probably think about their interests, goals, and abilities.
IV. Choosing an occupation in the field of nutrition services is an important decision to make.

Which one of the following is the BEST arrangement of these sentences?
A. II, IV, I, III   B. II, III, IV, I   C. IV, II, I, III   D. IV, II, III, I

KEY (CORRECT ANSWERS)

1. The correct answer is C.
Choice A conveys the incorrect impression that proper precautions caused a personal injury accident.
Choice B conveys the incorrect impression that proper precautions caused a personal injury accident.
Choice C best presents the original information: Martin Wilson failed to take proper precautions and this failure caused a personal injury accident.
Choice D states that Martin Wilson was in a personal injury accident. The original information states that Martin Wilson caused a personal injury accident, but it does not state that Martin Wilson was in a personal injury accident.

2. The correct answer is D.
Choices A and C present the information in the paragraph out of logical sequence. In both A and C, sentence I comes before sentence III. The key element in the organization of this paragraph is that sentence III contains the information to which sentence I refers; therefore, in logical sequence, sentence III should come before sentence I.
Choice B also presents the information in the paragraph out of logical sequence. Choice B places sentence IV in between sentence I and sentence III, thereby interrupting the logical sequence of the information in the paragraph.
Choice D presents the information in the paragraph in the best logical sequence. Sentence IV introduces the main idea of the paragraph: "choosing an occupation in the field of nutrition services." Sentences II, III, I then follow up on this idea by describing, in order, the steps involved in making such a choice. Choice D is the best answer to this sample question.

PREPARING WRITTEN MATERIAL
EXAMINATION SECTION
TEST 1

DIRECTIONS: Each short paragraph below is followed by four restatements or summaries of the information contained within it. Select the one that most completely and accurately restates the information given in the paragraph. *PRINT THE LETTER OF THE CORRECT ANSWER IN THE SPACE AT THE RIGHT.*

1. India's night jasmine, or hurshinghar, is different from most flowering plants, in that its flowers are closed during the day, and open after dark. The scientific reason for this is probably that the plant has avoided competing with other flowers for pollinating insects and birds, and relies instead on the service of nocturnal bats that are drawn to the flower's nectar. According to an old Indian legend, however, the flowers sprouted from the funeral ashes of a beautiful young girl who had fallen hopelessly in love with the sun.
    A. Despite the Indian legend that explains why the hurshinghar's flowers open at dusk, scientists believe it has to do with competition for available pollinators.
    B. The Indian hurshinghar's closure of its flowers during the day is due to a lack of available pollinators.
    C. The hurshinghar of India has evolved an unhealthy dependency on nocturnal bats.
    D. Like most myths, the Indian legend of the hurshinghar's night-flowering has been disproved by science.

1.____

2. Charles Lindbergh's trans-Atlantic flight from New York to Paris made him an international hero in 1927, but he lived nearly another fifty years, and by most accounts they weren't terribly happy ones. The two greatest tragedies of his life—the 1932 kidnapping and murder of his oldest son, and an unshakeable reputation as a Nazi sympathizer during World War II—he blamed squarely on the rabid media hounds who stalked his every move.
    A. Despite the fact that Charles Lindbergh had a hand in the two greatest tragedies of his life, he insisted on blaming the media for his problems.
    B. Charles Lindbergh lived a largely unhappy life after the glory of his 1927 trans-Atlantic flight, and he blamed his unhappiness on media attention
    C. Charles Lindbergh's later life was marked by despair and disillusionment.
    D. Because of the rabid media attention sparked by Charles Lindbergh's 1927 trans-Atlantic flight, he would later consider it the last happy event of his life

2.____

3. The United States, one of the world's youngest nations in the early twentieth century, had yet to spread its wings in terms of foreign affairs, preferring to remain isolated and opposed to meddling in the affairs of others. But the fact remained that as a young nation situated on the opposite side of the globe from Europe, Africa, and Asia, the United States had much work to do in

3.____

establishing relations with the rest of the world. So, too, as the European colonial powers continued to battle for influence in North and South America, did the United States come to believe that it was proper for them to keep these nations from encroaching into their sphere of influence.
   A. The roots of the Monroe Doctrine can be traced to the foreign policy shift of the United States during the early nineteenth century.
   B. In the early nineteenth century, the United States shifted its foreign policy to reflect a growing desire to actively protect its interests in the Western Hemisphere.
   C. In the early nineteenth century, the United States was too young and undeveloped to have devised much in the way of foreign policy.
   D. The United States adopted a more aggressive foreign policy in the early nineteenth century in order to become a diplomatic player on the world stage.

4. Hertha Ayrton, a nineteenth-century Englishwoman, pursued a career in science during a time when most women were not given the opportunity to go to college. Her series of successes led to her induction into the Institution of Electrical Engineers in 1899, when she was the first woman to receive this professional honor. Her most noted accomplishment was the research and invention of an anti-gas fan that the British War Office used in the trench warfare of World War I.
   A. The British Army's success in World War I can be partly attributed to Hertha Ayrton, a groundbreaking British scientist.
   B. Hertha Ayrton was the first woman to be inducted into the Institution of Electrical Engineers.
   C. The injustices of nineteenth-century England were no match for the brilliant mind of Hertha Ayrton.
   D. Hertha Ayrton defied the restrictions of her society by building a successful scientific career.

4._____

5. Scientists studying hyenas in Tanzania's Ngorongoro Crater have observed that hyena clans have evolved a system of territoriality that allows each clan a certain space to hunt within the 100-square-mile area. These territories are not marked by natural boundaries, but by droppings and excretions from the hyenas' scent glands. Usually, the hyenas take these boundary lines very seriously; some hyena clans have been observed abandoning their pursuit of certain prey after the prey has crossed into another territory, even though no members of the neighboring clan are anywhere in sight.
   A. The hyenas of Ngorongoro Crater illustrate that the best way to peacefully co-exist within a limited territory is to strictly delineate and defend territorial borders.
   B. While most territorial boundaries are marked using geographical features, the hyenas of Ngorongoro Crater have devised another method.
   C. The hyena clans of Ngorongoro Crater, in order to co-exist within a limited hunting territory, have developed a method of marking strict territorial boundaries.
   D. As with most species, the hyenas of Ngorongoro Crater have proven the age-old motto: "To the victor go the spoils."

5._____

3 (#1)

6. The flood control policy of the U.S. Army Corps of Engineers has long been an obvious feature of the American landscape—the Corps seeks to contain the nation's rivers with an enormous network of dams and levees, "channelizing" rivers into small, confined routes that will stay clear of settled flood—plains when rivers rise. As a command of the U.S. Army, the Corps seems to have long seen the nation's rivers as an enemy to be fought; one of the agency's early training films speaks of the Corps' "battle" with its adversary, Mother Nature.

6.____

   A. The dams and levees built by the U.S. Army Corps of Engineers have at least defeated their adversary, Mother Nature.
   B. The flood control policy of the U.S. Army Corps of Engineers has often reflected a military point of view, making the nation's rivers into enemies that must be defeated.
   C. When one realizes that the flood policy of the U.S. Army Corps of Engineers has always relied on a kind of military strategy, it is only possible to view the Corps' efforts as a failure.
   D. By damming and channelizing the nation's rivers, the U.S. Army Corps of Engineers have made America's flood plains safe for farming and development.

7. Frogs with extra legs or missing legs have been showing up with greater frequency over the past decade, and scientists have been baffled by the cause. Some researchers have concluded that pesticide runoff from farms is to blame; others say a common parasite, the trematode, is the culprit. Now, a new study suggests that both these factors in combination have disturbed normal development in many frogs, leading to the abnormalities.

7.____

   A. Despite several studies, scientists still have no idea what is causing the widespread incidence of deformities among aquatic frogs.
   B. In the debate over what is causing the increase in frog deformities, environmentalists tend to blame pesticide runoff, while others blame a common parasite, the trematode.
   C. A recent study suggests that both pesticide runoff and natural parasites have contributed to the increasing rate of deformities in frogs.
   D. Because of their aquatic habitat, frogs are among the most susceptible organisms to chemical ad environmental change, and this is illustrated by the increasing rate of physical deformities among frog populations.

8. The builders of the Egyptian pyramids, to insure that each massive structure was built on a completely flat surface, began by cutting a network of criss-crossing channels into the pyramid's mapped-out ground space and partly filling the channels with water. Because the channels were all interconnected, the water was distributed evenly throughout the channel system, and all the workers had to do to level their building surface was cut away any rock above the waterline.

8.____

   A. The modern carpenter's level uses a principle that was actually invented several centuries ago by the builders of the Egyptian pyramids.
   B. The discovery of the ancient Egyptians' sophisticated construction techniques is a quiet argument against the idea that they were built by slaves.

C. The use of water to insure that the pyramids were level mark the Egyptians as one of the most scientifically advanced of the ancient civilizations.
D. The builders of the Egyptian pyramids used a simple but ingenious method for ensuring a level building surface with interconnected channels of water

9. Thunderhead Mountain, a six-hundred-foot-high formation of granite in the Black Hills of South Dakota, is slowly undergoing a transformation that will not be finished for more than a century, when what remains of the mountain will have become the largest sculpture in the world. The statue, begun in 1947 by a Boston Sculptor named Henry Ziolkowski, is still being carved and blasted by his wife and children into the likeness of Crazy Horse, the legendary chief of the Sioux tribe of American natives. The enormity of the sculpture—the planned length of one of the figure's arms is 263 feet—is understandable, given the historical greatness of Crazy Horse.
   A. Only a hero as great as Crazy Horse could warrant a sculpture so large that it will take morae than a century to complete.
   B. In 1947, sculptor Henry Ziolkowski began work on what he imagined would be the largest sculpture in the world—even though he knew he would not live to see it completed.
   C. The huge Black Hills sculpture of the great Sioux chief Crazy Horse, still being carried out by the family of Henry Ziolkowski, will some day be the largest sculpture in the world.
   D. South Dakota's Thunderhead Mountain will soon be the site of the world's largest sculpture, a statue of the Sioux chief Crazy Horse.

9.____

10. Because they were some of the first explorers to venture into the western frontier of North America, the French were responsible for the naming of several native tribes. Some of these names were poorly conceived—the worst of which was perhaps Eskimo, the name for the natives of the far North, which translates roughly as "eaters of raw flesh." The name is incorrect; these people have always cooked their fish and game, and they now call themselves the Inuit, a native term that means "the people."
   A. The first to explore much of North America's western frontier were the French, and they usually gave improper or poorly-informed names to the native tribes.
   B. The Eskimos of North America have never eaten raw flesh, so it is curious that the French would give them a name that means "eaters of raw flesh."
   C. The Inuit have fought for many years to overcome the impression that they eat raw flesh.
   D. Like many native tribes, the Inuit were once incorrectly named by French explorers, but they have since corrected the mistake themselves.

10.____

11. Of the 30,000 species of spiders worldwide, only a handful are dangerous to human beings, but this doesn't prevent many people from having a powerful fear of all spiders, whether they are venomous or not. The leading scientific theory about arachnophobia, as this fear is known, is that far in our evolutionary past, some species of spider must have presented a serious enough threat to people that the sight of a star-shaped body or an eight-legged walk was coded into our genes as a danger signal.   11.____
    A. Scientists theorize that peoples' widespread fear of spiders can be traced to an ancient spider species that was dangerous enough to trigger this fearful reaction.
    B. The fear known as arachnophobia is triggered by the sight of a star-shaped body or an eight-legged walk.
    C. Because most spiders have a uniquely shaped body that triggers a human fear response, many humans are afflicted with the fear of spiders known as arachnophobia.
    D. Though only a few of the planet's 30,000 spider species are dangerous to people, many people have an unreasonable fear of them.

12. From the 1970s to the 1990s, the percentage of Americans living in the suburbs climbed from 37% to 47%. In the latter part of the 1990s, a movement emerged that questioned the good of such a population shift—or at least, the good of the speed and manner in which this suburban land was being developed. Often, people began to argue, the planning of such growth was flawed, resulting in a phenomenon that has become known as suburban "sprawl," or the growth of suburban orbits around cities at rates faster than infrastructures could support, and in ways that are damaging to the environment   12.____
    A. The term "urban sprawl" was coined in the 1990s, when the movement against unchecked suburban development began to gather momentum.
    B. In the 1980s and 1990s, home builders benefited from a boom in their most favored demographic segment, suburban new home buyers.
    C. Suburban development tends to suffer from poor planning, which can lead to a lower quality of life for residents
    D. The surge in suburban residences in the late twentieth century was criticized by many as "sprawl" that could not be supported by existing resources

13. Medicare, a $200 billion-a-year program, processes 1 billion claims annually, and in the year 2000, the computer system that handles these claims came under criticism. The General Accounting Office branded Medicare's financial management system as outdated and inadequate—one in a series of studies and reports warning that the program is plagued with duplication, overcharges, double billings, and confusion among users.   13.____
    A. The General Accounting Office's 2000 report proves that Medicare is bloated bureaucracy in need of substantial reform.
    B. Medicare's confusing computer network is an example of how the federal government often neglects the programs that mean the most to average American citizens.

C. In the year 2000, the General Accounting Office criticized Medicare's financial accounting network as inefficient and outdated.
D. Because it has to handle so many claims each year, Medicare's financial accounting system often produces redundancies and errors.

14. The earliest known writing materials were thin clay tablets, used in Mesopotamia more than 5,000 years ago. Although the tablets were cheap and easy to produce, they had two major disadvantages: they were difficult to store, and once the clay had dried and hardened, a person could not write on them. The ancient Egyptians later discovered a better writing material—the thin bark of the papyrus reed, a plant that grew near the mouth of the Nile River, which could be peeled into long strips, woven into a mat-like layer, pounded flat with heavy mallets, and then dried in the sun.   14.____
    A. The Egyptians, after centuries of frustration with clay writing tablets, were finally forced to invent a better writing surface.
    B. With the bark of the papyrus reed, ancient Egyptians made a writing material that overcame the disadvantages of clay tablets.
    C. The Egyptian invention of the papyrus scroll was necessitated in part by a relative lack of available clay.
    D. The word "paper" can be traced to the innovations of the Egyptians, who made the first paper-like writing material from the bark of papyrus plant.

15. In 1850, the German pianomaker Heinrich Steinweg and his family stepped off an immigrant ship in New York City, threw themselves into competition with dozens of other established craftsmen, and defeated them all by reinventing the instrument. The company they created commanded the market for nearly the next century and a half, while their competitors—some of the most acclaimed pianomakers in the business—faded into obscurity. And all the while, Steinway & Sons, through their sponsorship and encouragement of the world's most distinguished pianists, helped define the cultural life of the young United States.   15.____
    A. The Steinways capitalized on weak competition during the mid-nineteenth century to capture the American piano market.
    B. Because of their technical and cultural innovations, the Steinways had an advantage over other American pianomakers.
    C. Heinrich Steinweg founded the Steinway piano empire in 1850.
    D. From humble immigrant origins, the Steinway family rose to dominate both the pianomaking industry and American musical culture.

16. Feng Shui, the ancient Chinese science of studying the natural environment's effect on a person's well-being, has gained new popularity in the design and decoration of buildings. Although a complex area of study, a basic premise of Feng Shui is that each building creates a unique field of energy which affects the inhabitants of that building or home. In recent years, decorators and realtors have begun to offer services which include a diagnosis of a building's Feng Shui, or energy.   16.____
    A. Feng Shui, the Chinese science of balancing environmental energies, has been given more aesthetic quality by recent practitioners.

B. Generally, practitioners of Feng Shui work to create balance within a room, carefully arranging sharp and soft surfaces to create a positive environment that suits the room's primary purpose.
C. The idea behind the Chinese "science" of Feng Sui objects give off certain energies that affect a building's inhabitants has been a difficult one for most Westerners to accept, but it is gaining in popularity.
D. The ancient Chinese science of Feng Shui, which studies the balance of energies in a person's environment, has become popular among those who design and decorate buildings.

17. Because the harsh seasonal variations of the Kansas plains make survival difficult for most plant life, the area is dominated by tall, sturdy grasses. The only tree that has been able to survive and prosper throughout the wide expanse of prairie is the cottonwood, which can take root and grow in the most extreme climatic conditions. Sometimes a storm will shear off a living branch and carry it downstream, where it may snag along a sandbar and take root. 17.____
    A. Among the plant life of the Kansas plains, the only tree is the cottonwood.
    B. The only prosperous tree on the Kansas plains is the cottonwood, which can take root and grow in a wide range of conditions.
    C. Only the cottonwood, whose branches can grow after being broken off and washed down a river, is capable of surviving the climatic extremes of the Kansas plains.
    D. Because it is the most widespread and hardiest tree on the Kansas plains, the cottonwood had become a symbol of pioneer grit and fortitude.

18. In the twenty-first century, it's easy to see the automobile as the keystone of American popular culture. Subtract linen dusters, driving goggles, and women's *crepe de chine* veils from our history, and you've taken the Roaring out of the Twenties. Take away the ducktail haircuts, pegged pants, and upturned collars from the teen Car Cult of the Fifties, and the decade isn't nearly as Fabulous. Were the chromed and tailfinned muscle cars of the automobile' Golden Age modeled after us, or were we mimicking them? 18.____
    A. Ever since its invention, the automobile has shaped American culture.
    B. Many of the familiar names we give historical era, such as "Roaring Twenties" and "Fabulous Fifties," were given because of the predominance of the automobile.
    C. Americans' tastes in clothing have been determined primarily by the cars they drive.
    D. Teenagers have had a fascination for automobiles ever since the motorcar was first invented.

19. Since the 1960s, an important issue for Canada has been the status of minority French-speaking Canadians, especially in the province of Quebec, whose inhabitants make up 30% of the Canadian population and trace their ancestry back to a Canada that preceded British influence. In response to pressure from Quebec nationalists, the government in 1982 added a Charter of Rights to the constitution, restoring important rights that dated back to the time of aboriginal treaties. Separatism is still a prominent issue, though successive 19.____

referendums and constitutional inquiries have not resulted in any realistic progress toward Quebec's independence.
- A. Despite the fact that Quebec's inhabitants have their roots in Canada's original settlers, they have been constantly oppressed by the descendants of those who came later, the British.
- B. It seems unavoidable that Quebec's linguistic and cultural differences with the rest of Canada will some day lead to its secession.
- C. French-speaking Quebec's activism over the last several decades has led to concessions by the Canadian government, but it seems that Quebec will remain a part of the country for some time.
- D. The inhabitants of Quebec are an aboriginal culture that has been exploited by the Canadian government for years, but they are gradually winning back their rights.

20. For years, musicians and scientists have tried to discover what it is about an eighteenth-century Stradivarius violin—which may sell for more than $1 million on today's market—that gives it its unique sound. In 1977, American scientist Joseph Nagyvary discovered that the Stradivarius is made of a spruce wood that came from Venice, where timber was stored beneath the sea, and unlike the dry-seasoned wood from which other violins were made, this spruce contains microscopic holes which add resonance to the violin's sound. Nagyvary also found the varnish used on the Stradivarius to be equally unique, containing tiny mineral crystals that appear to have come from ground-up gemstones, which would filter out high-pitched tones and give the violin a smoother sound. 20.____
- A. After carefully studying Stradivarius violins to discover the source of their unique sound, an American scientist discovered two qualities in the construction of them that set them apart from other instruments: the wood from which they were made, and the varnish used to coat the wood.
- B. The two qualities that give the Stradivarius violin such a unique sound are the wood, which adds resonance, and the finish, which filters out high-pitched tones.
- C. The Stradivarius violin, because of the unique wood and finish used in its construction, is widely regarded as the finest string instrument ever manufactured in the world.
- D. A close study of the Stradivarius violin has revealed that the best wood for making violins is Venetian spruce, stored underwater.

21. People who watch the display of fireflies on a clear summer evening are actually witnessing a complex chemical reaction called "bioluminescence," which turns certain organisms into living light bulbs. Organisms that produce this light undergo a reaction in which oxygen combines with a chemical called lucerfin and an enzyme called luciferase. Depending on the organism, the light produced from this reaction can range from the light green of the firefly to the bright red spots of a railroad worm. 21.____
- A. Although the function of most displays of bioluminescence is to attract mates, as is the case with fireflies, other species rely on bioluminescence for different purposes.

B. Bioluminescence, a phenomenon produced by several organisms, is the result of a chemical reaction that takes place within the body of the organism.
C. Of all the organisms in the world, only insects are capable of displaying bioluminescence.
D. Despite the fact that some organisms display bioluminescence, these reactions produce almost no heat, which is why the light they create is sometimes referred to as cold light.

22. The first of America's "log cabin" presidents, Andrew Jackson rose from humble backcountry origins to become a U.S. congressman and senator, a renowned military hero, and the seventh president of the United States. Among many Americans, especially those of the western frontier, he was acclaimed as a symbol of the "new" American: self-made, strong through closeness to nature, and endowed with a powerful moral courage.

    22.____

    A. Andrew Jackson was the first American president to rise from modest origins.
    B. Because he was born poor, President Andrew Jackson was more popular among Americans of the western frontier.
    C. Andrew Jackson's humble background, along with his outstanding achievements, made him into a symbol of American strength and self-sufficiency.
    D. Andrew Jackson achieved success as a legislator, soldier, and president because he was born humbly and had to work for every honor he ever received.

23. In the past few decades, while much of the world's imagination has focused on the possibilities of outer space, some scientists have been exploring a different frontier—the ocean floor. Although ships have been sailing the oceans for centuries, only recently have scientists developed vehicles strong enough to sustain the pressure of deep-sea exploration and observation. These fiberglass vehicles, called submersibles, are usually just big enough to take two or three people to the deepest parts of the oceans' floors.

    23.____

    A. Modern submersible vehicles, thanks to recent technological innovations, are now exploring underwater cliffs, crevices, and mountain ranges that were once unreachable.
    B. While most people tend to fantasize about exploring outer space, they should be turning toward a more accessible realm—the depths of the earth's oceans.
    C. Because of the necessarily small size of submersible vehicles, exploration of the deep ocean is not a widespread activity.
    D. Recent technological developments have helped scientists to turn their attention from deep space to the deep ocean.

24. The panda—a native of the remote mountainous regions of China—subsists almost entirely on the tender shoots of the bamboo plant. This restrictive diet has allowed the panda to evolve an anatomical structure that is completely different from that of other bears, whose paws are aligned for running, stabbing, and scratching. The panda's paw has an over-developed wrist bone that juts out below the other claws like a thumb, and the panda uses this "thumb" to grip bamboo shoots while it strips them of their leaves.

   A. The panda is the only bear-like animal that feeds on vegetation, and it has a kind of thumb to help it grip bamboo shoots.
   B. The panda's limited diet of bamboo has led it to evolve a thumb-like appendage for grasping bamboo shoots.
   C. The panda's thumb-like appendage is a factor that limits its diet to the shoots of the bamboo plant.
   D. Because bamboo shoots must be held tightly while eaten, the panda's thumb-like appendage ensure that it is the only bear-like animal that eats bamboo.

24._____

25. The stability and security of the Balkan region remains a primary concern for Greece in post-Cold War Europe, and Greece's active participation in peacekeeping and humanitarian operations in Georgia, Albania, and Bosnia are substantial examples of this commitment. Due to its geopolitical position, Greece believes it necessary to maintain, at least for now, a more nationalized defense force than other European nations. It is Greece's hope that the new spirit of integration and cooperation will help establish a common European foreign affairs and defense policy that might ease some of these regional tensions, and allow a greater level of Greek participation in NATO's integrated military structure.

   A. Greece's proximity to the unstable Balkan region has led it to keep a more nationalized military, though it hopes to become more involved in a common European defense force.
   B. The Balkan states present a greater threat to Greece than any other European nation, and Greece has adopted a highly nationalist military force as a result.
   C. Greece, the only Balkan state to belong to NATO, has an isolationist approach to defense, but hopes to achieve greater integration in the organization's combined forces.
   D. Greece's failure to become more militarily integrated with the rest of Europe can be attributed to the failure to establish a common European defense policy.

25._____

KEY (CORRECT ANSWERS)

1. A
2. B
3. B
4. D
5. C

6. B
7. C
8. D
9. C
10. D

11. A
12. D
13. C
14. B
15. D

16. D
17. B
18. A
19. C
20. A

21. B
22. C
23. D
24. B
25. A

PREPARING WRITTEN MATERIAL

PARAGRAPH REARRANGEMENT
COMMENTARY

The sentences that follow are in scrambled order. You are to rearrange them in proper order and indicate the letter choice containing the correct answer at the space at the right.

Each group of sentences in this section is actually a paragraph presented in scrambled order. Each sentence in the group has a place in that paragraph; no sentence is to be left out. You are to read each group of sentences and decide upon the best order in which to put the sentences so as to form a well-organized paragraph.

The questions in this section measure the ability to solve a problem when all the facts relevant to its solution are not given.

More specifically, certain positions of responsibility and authority require the employee to discover connection between events sometimes, apparently, unrelated. In order to do this, the employee will find it necessary to correctly infer that unspecified events have probably occurred or are likely to occur. This ability becomes especially important when action must be taken on incomplete information.

Accordingly, these questions require competitors to choose among several suggested alternatives, each of which presents a different sequential arrangement of the events. Competitors must choose the MOST logical of the suggested sequences.

In order to do so, they may be required to draw on general knowledge to infer missing concepts or events that are essential to sequencing the given events. Competitors should be careful to infer only what is essential to the sequence. The plausibility of the wrong alternatives will always require the inclusion of unlikely events or of additional chains of events which are NOT essential to sequencing the given events.

It's very important to remember that you are looking for the best of the four possible choices, and that the best choice of all may not even be one of the answers you're given to choose from.

There is no one right way to solve these problems. Many people have found it helpful to first write out the order of the sentences, as they would have arranged them, on their scrap paper before looking at the possible answers. If their optimum answer is there, this can save them some time. If it isn't, this method can still give insight into solving the problem. Others find it most helpful to just go through each of the possible choices, contrasting each as they go along. You should use whatever method feels comfortable and works for you.

While most of these types of questions are not that difficult, we've added a higher percentage of the difficult type, just to give you more practice. Usually there are only one or two questions on this section that contain such subtle distinctions that you're unable to answer confidently. And you then may find yourself stuck deciding between two possible choices, neither of which you're sure about.

PREPARING WRITTEN MATERIAL
PARAGRAPH REARRANGEMENT
EXAMINATION SECTION
TEST 1

DIRECTIONS: The following groups of sentences need to be arranged in an order that makes sense. Select the letter preceding the sequence that represents the best sentence order. *PRINT THE LETTER OF THE CORRECT ANSWER IN THE SPACE AT THE RIGHT.*

1. I. The ostrich egg shell's legendary toughness makes it an excellent substitute for certain types of dishes or dinnerware, and in parts of Africa ostrich shells are cut and decorated for use as containers for water.
    II. Since prehistoric times, people have used the enormous egg of the ostrich as a part of their diet, a practice which has required much patience and hard work—to hard boil an ostrich egg takes about four hours.
    III. Opening the egg's shell, which is rock hard and nearly an inch thick, requires heavy tools, such as a saw or chisel; from inside, a baby ostrich must use a hornlike projection on its beak as a miniature pick-axe to escape from the egg.
    IV. The offspring of all higher-order animals originate from single egg cells that are carried by mothers, and most of these eggs are relatively small, often microscopic.
    V. The egg of the African ostrich, however, weighs a massive thirty pounds, making it the largest single cell on earth, and a common object of human curiosity and wonder.
    The BEST order is:
    A. V, IV, I, II, III   B. I, IV, V, III, II   C. IV, II, III, V, I   D. IV, V, II, III, I

    1.____

2. I. Typically only a few feet high on the open sea, individual tsunami have been known to circle the entire globe two or three times if their progress is not interrupted, but are not usually dangerous until they approach the shallow water that surrounds land masses.
    II. Some of the most terrifying and damaging hazards caused by earthquakes are tsunami, which were once called "tidal waves"—a poorly chosen name, since these waves have nothing to do with tides.
    III. Then a wave, slowed by the sudden drag on the lower part of its moving water column, will pile upon itself, sometimes reaching a height of over 100 feet.
    IV. Tsunami (Japanese for "great harbor wave") are seismic waves that are caused by earthquakes near oceanic trenches, and once triggered, can travel up to 600 miles an hour on the open ocean.
    V. A land-shoaling tsunami is capable of extraordinary destruction; some tsunami have deposited large boats miles inland, washed out two-foot-thick seawalls, and scattered locomotive trains over long distances.
    The BEST order is:
    A. IV, I, III, II, V   B. I, III, IV, II, V   C. V, I, III, II, IV   D. II, IV, I, III, V

    2.____

3. I. Soon, by the 1940s, jazz was the most popular type of music among American intellectuals and college students.
    II. In the early days of jazz, it was considered "lowdown" music, or music that was played only in rough, disreputable bars and taverns.
    III. However, jazz didn't take too long to develop from early ragtime melodies into more complex, sophisticated forms, such as Charlie Parker's "bebop" style of jazz.
    IV. After charismatic band leaders such as Duke Ellington and Count Basie brought jazz to a larger audience, and jazz continued to evolve into more complicated forms, white audiences began to accept and even to enjoy the new American art form.
    V. Many white Americans, who then dictated the tastes of society, were wary of music that was played almost exclusively in black clubs in the poorer sections of cities and towns.
    The BEST order is:
    A. V, IV, III, II, I   B. II, V, III, IV, I   C. IV, V, III, I, II   D. I, II, IV, III, V

3.____

4. I. Then, hanging in a windless place, the magnetized end of the needle would always point to the south.
    II. The needle could then be balanced on the rim of a cup, or the edge of a fingernail, but this balancing act was hard to maintain, and the needle often fell off.
    III. Other needles would point to the north, and it was important for any traveler finding his way with a compass to remember which kind of magnetized needle he was carrying.
    IV. To make some of the earliest compasses in recorded history, ancient Chinese "magicians" would rub a needle with a piece of magnetized iron called a lodestone.
    V. A more effective method of keeping the needle free to swing with its magnetic pull was to attach a strand of silk to the center of the needle with a tiny piece of wax.
    The BEST order is:
    A. IV, II, V, I, III   B. IV, III, V, II, I   C. IV, V, II, I, III   D. IV, I, III, V, II

4.____

5. I The now-famous first mate of the *H.M.S. Bounty*, Fletcher Christian, founded one of the world's most peculiar civilizations in 1790.
    II. The men knew they had just committed a crime for which they could be hanged, so they set sail for Pitcairn, a remote, abandoned island in the far eastern region of the Polynesian archipelago, accompanied by twelve Polynesian women and six men.
    III. In a mutiny that has become legendary, Christian and the others forced Captain Bligh into a lifeboat and set him adrift off the coast of Tonga in April of 1789.
    IV. In early 1790, the *Bounty* landed at Pitcairn Island, where the men lived out the rest of their lives and founded an isolated community which to this day includes direct descendants of Christian and the other Crewmen.

5.____

V. The *Bounty*, commanded by Captain William Bligh, was in the middle of a global voyage, and Christian and his shipmates had come to the conclusion that Bligh was a reckless madman who would lead them to their deaths unless they took the ship from him.

The BEST order is:
A. IV, V, III, II, I   B. I, III, V, II, IV   C. I, V, III, II, IV   D. III, I, V, IV, II

6. I. But once the vines had been led to make orchids, the flowers had to be carefully hand-pollinated, because unpollinated orchids usually lasted less than a day, wilting and dropping off the vine before it had even become dark.
   II. The Totonac farmers discovered that looping a vine back around once it reached a five-foot height on its host tree would cause the vine to flower.
   III. Though they knew how to process the fruit pods and extract vanilla's flavoring agent, the Totonacs also knew that a wild vanilla vine did not produce abundant flowers or fruit.
   IV. Wild vines climbed along the trunks and canopies of trees, and this constant upward growth diverted most of the vine's energy to making leaves instead of the orchid flowers that once pollinated, would produce the flavorful pods.
   V. Hundreds of years before vanilla became a prized food flavoring in Europe and the Western World, the Totonac Indians of the Mexican Gulf Coast were skilled cultivators of the vanilla vine, whose fruit they literally worshipped as a goddess.

   The BEST order is:
   A. II, III, IV, I, V   B. II, IV, III, I, V   C. V, III, IV, II, I   D. III, IV, I, II, V

7. I. Once airborne, the spider is at the mercy of the air currents—usually the spider takes a brief journey, traveling close to the ground, but some have been found in air samples collected as high as 10,000 feet, or been reported landing on ships far out at sea.
   II. Once a young spider has hatched, it must leave the environment into which it was born as quickly as possible, in order to avoid competing with its hundreds of brothers and sisters for food.
   III. The silk rises into warm air currents, and as soon as the pull feels adequate the spider lets go and drifts up into the air, suspended from the silk strand in the same way that a person might parasail.
   IV. To help young spiders do this, many species have adapted a practice known as "aerial dispersal," or, in common speech, "ballooning."
   V. A spider that wants to leave its surroundings quickly will climb to the top of a grass system or twig, face into the wind, and aim its back end into the air, releasing a long stream of silk from the glands near the tip of its abdomen.

   The BEST order is:
   A. V, IV, II, III, I   B. V, II, IV, I, III   C. II, V, IV, III, I   D. II, IV, V, III, I

8.
I. For about a year, Tycho worked at a castle in Prague with a scientist named Johannes Kepler, but their association was cut short by another argument that drove Kepler out of the castle, to later develop, on his own, the theory of planetary orbits.
II. Tycho found life without a nose embarrassing, so he made a new nose for himself out of silver, which reportedly remained glued to his face for the rest of his life.
III. Tycho Brahe, the 17th-century Danish astronomer, is today more famous for his odd and arrogant personality than for any contribution he has made to our knowledge of the stars and planets.
IV. Early in his career, as a student at Rostock University, Tycho got into an argument with another student about who was the better mathematician, and the two became so angry that the argument turned into a sword fight, during which Tycho's nose was sliced off.
V. Later in his life, Tycho's arrogance may have kept him from playing a part in one of the greatest astronomical discoveries in history: the elliptical orbits of the solar system's planets.

The BEST order is:
A. I, IV, II, III, V   B. IV, II, III, V, I   C. IV, II, I, III, V   D. III, IV, II, V, I

9.
I. The processionaries are so used to this routine that if a person picks up the end of a silk line and brings it back to the origin—creating a closed circle—the caterpillars may travel around and around for days, sometimes starving or freezing, without changing course.
II. Rather than relying on sight or sound, the other caterpillars, who are lined up end-to-end behind the leader, travel to and from their nests by walking on this silk line, and each will reinforce it by laying down its own marking line as it passes over.
III. In order to insure the safety of individuals, the processionary caterpillar nests in a tree with dozens of other caterpillars, and at night, when it is safest, they all leave together in search of food.
IV. The processionary caterpillar of the European continent is a perfect illustration of how much some inspect species rely on instinct in their daily routines.
V. As they leave their nests, the processionaries form a single-file line behind a leader who spins and lays out a silk line to mark the chosen path.

The BEST order is:
A. IV, III, V, II, I   B. III, V, IV, II, I   C. III, V, II, I, IV   D. IV, V, III, I, II

10.
I. Often, the child is also given a handcrafted walker or push cart, to provide support for its first upright explorations.
II. In traditional Indian families, a child's first steps are celebrated as a ceremonial event, rooted in ancient myth.
III. These carts are often intricately designed to resemble the chariot of Krishna, an important figure in Indian mythology.
IV. The sound of these anklet bells is intended to mimic the footsteps of the legendary child Rama, who is celebrated in devotional songs throughout India.

V. When the child's parents see that the child is ready to begin walking, they will fit it with specially designed ankle bracelets, adorned with gently ringing bells.

The BEST order is:
A. II, III, IV, I, V   B. II, V, III, I, IV   C. V, IV, I, III, II   D. V, III, II, I, IV

11. I. The settlers planted Osage oranges all across Middle America, and today long lines and rectangles of Osage orange trees can still be seen on the prairies, running along the former boundaries of farms that no longer exist.
II. After trying sod walls and water-filled ditches with no success, American farmers began to look for a plant that was adaptable to prairie weather, and that could be trimmed into a hedge that was "pig-tight, horse-high, and bull-strong."
III. The tree, so named because it bore a large (but inedible) fruit the size of an orange, was among the sturdiest and hardiest of American trees, and was prized among Native Americans for the strength and flexibility of bows which were made from its wood.
IV. The first people to practice agriculture on the American flatlands were faced with an important problem: what would they use to fence their land in a place that was almost entirely without trees or rocks?
V. Finally, an Illinois farmer brought the settlers a tree that was native to the land between the Red and Arkansas rivers, a tree called the Osage orange.

The BEST order is:
A. II, I, V, III, IV   B. I, II, III, IV, V   C. IV, II, V, III, I   D. IV, II, I, III, V

11.____

12. I. After about ten minutes of such spirited and complicated activity, the head dancer is free to make up his or her own movements while maintaining the interest of the New Year's crowd.
II. The dancer will then perform a series of leg kicks, while at the same time operating the lion's mouth with his own hand and moving the ears and eyes by means of a string which is attached to the dancer's own mouth.
III. The most difficult role of this dance belongs to the one who controls the lion's head; this person must lead all the other "parts" of the lion through the choreographed segments of the dance.
IV. The head dancer begins with a complex series of steps. alternately stepping forward with the head raised, and then retreating a few steps while lowering the head, a movement that is intended to create the impression that the lion is keeping a watchful eye for anything evil.
V. When performing a traditional Chinese New Year's lion dance, several performers must fit themselves inside a large lion costume and work together to enact different parts of the dance.

The BEST order is:
A. V, III, IV, II, I   B. III, IV, II, V, I   C. III, I, V, IV, II   D. IV, II, III, V, I

12.____

13.
   I. For many years the shell of the chambered nautilus was treasured in Europe for its beauty and intricacy, but collectors were unaware that they were in possession of the structure that marked a "missing link" in the evolution of marine mollusks.
   II. The nautilus, however, evolved a series of enclosed chambers in its shell, and invented a new use for the structure: the shell began to serve as a buoyancy device.
   III. Equipped with this new flotation device, the nautilus did not need the single, muscular foot of its predecessors, but instead developed flaps, tentacles, and a gentle form of jet propulsion that transformed it into the first mollusk able to take command of its own density and explore a three-dimensional world.
   IV. By pumping and adjusting air pressure into the chambers, the nautilus could spend the day resting on the bottom, and then rise toward the surface at night in search of food.
   V. The nautilus shell looks like a large snail shell, similar to those of its ancestors, who used their shells as protective coverings while they were anchored to the sea floor.
   The BEST order is:
   A. V, II, IV, I, III   B. V, I, II, III, IV   C. I, II, V, III, IV   D. I, V, II, IV, III   13.____

14.
   I. While France and England battled for control of the region, the Acadiens prospered on the fertile farmland, which was finally secured by England in 1713.
   II. Early in the 17th century, settlers from Western France founded a colony called Acadie in what is now the Canadian province of Nova Scotia.
   III. At this time, English officials feared the presence of spies among the Acadiens who might be loyal to their French homeland, and the Acadiens were deported to spots along the Atlantic and Caribbean shores of America.
   IV. The French settlers remained on this land, under English rule, for around forty years, until the beginning of the French and Indian War, another conflict between France and England.
   V. As the Acadien refugees drifted toward a final home in Southern Louisiana, neighbors shortened their name to "Cadien," and finally "Cajun," the name which the descendants of early Acadiens still call themselves.
   The BEST order is:
   A. I, IV, II, III, V   B. II, I, III, V, IV   C. II, I, IV, III, V   D. V, II, III, IV, I   14.____

15.
   I. Traditional households in the Eastern and Western regions of Africa serve two meals a day—one at around noon, and the other in the evening.
   II. The starch is then used in the way that Americans might use a spoon, to scoop up a portion of the main dish on the person's plate.
   III. The reason for the starch's inclusion in every meal has to do with taste as well as nutrition; African food can be very spicy, and the starch is known to cool the burning effect of the main dish.
   IV. When serving these meals, the main dish is usually served on individual plates, and the starch is served on a communal plate, from which diners break off a piece of bread or scoop rice or fufu in their fingers.   15.____

V. The typical meals usually consist of a thick stew or soup as the main course, and an accompanying starch—either bread, rice, or *fufu*, a starchy grain paste similar in consistency to mashed potatoes.
The BEST order is:
A. V, II, III, IV, I B. V, I, IV, III, II C. I, IV, V, III, II D. I, V, IV, II, III

16. I. In the early days of the American Midwest, Indiana settlers sometimes came together to hold an event called an apple peeling, where neighboring settlers gathered at the homestead of a host family to help prepare the hosts' apple crop for cooking, canning, and making apple butter.
    II. At the beginning of the event, each peeler sat down in front of a ten- or twenty-gallon stone jar and was given a crock of apples and a paring knife.
    III. Once a peeler had finished with a crock, another was placed next to him; if the peeler was an unmarried man, he kept a strict count of the number of apples he had peeled, because the winner was allowed to kiss the girl of his choice.
    IV. The peeling usually ended by 9:30 in the evening, when the neighbors gathered in the host family's parlor for a dance social.
    V. The apples were peeled, cored, and quartered, and then placed into the jar.
    The BEST order is:
    A. I, V, III, IV, II B. II, V, III, IV, I C. I, II, V, III, IV D. II, I, V, IV, III

16._____

17. I. If your pet turtle is a land turtle and is native to temperate climates, it will stop eating some time in October, which should be your cue to prepare the turtle for hibernation.
    II. The box should then be covered with a wire screen, which will protect the turtle from any rodents or predators that might want to take advantage of a motionless and helpless animal.
    III. When your turtle hasn't eaten for a while and appears ready to hibernate, it should be moved to its winter quarters, most likely a cellar or garage, where the temperature should range between 40° and 45°F.
    IV. Instead of feeding the turtle, you should bathe it every day in warm water, to encourage the turtle to empty its intestines in preparation for its long winter sleep.
    V. Here the turtle should be placed in a well-ventilated box whose bottom is covered with a moisture-absorbing layer of clay beads, and then filled three-fourths full with almost dry peat moss or wood chips, into which the turtle will burrow and sleep for several months.
    The BEST order is:
    A. I, IV, III, V, II B. III, IV, II, V, I C. III, II, IV, I, V D. IV, V, II, III, I

17._____

18. I. Once he has reached the nest, the hunter uses two sturdy bamboo poles like huge chopsticks to pull the next away from the mountainside, into a large basket that will be lowered to people waiting below.
    II. The world's largest honeybees colonize the Nealese mountainsides, building honeycombs as large as a person on sheer rock faces that are often hundreds of feet high.

18._____

III. In the remote mountain country of Nepal, a small band of "honey hunters" carry out a tradition so ancient that 10,000 year-old drawings of the practice have been found in the caves of Nepal.
IV. To harvest the honey and beeswax from these combs, a honey hunter climbs above the nests, lowers a long bamboo-fiber ladder over the cliff, and then climbs down.
V. Throughout this dangerous practice, the hunter is stung repeatedly, and only the veterans, with skin that has been toughened over the years, are able to return from a hunt without the painful swelling caused by stings.

The BEST order is:
A. II, IV, III, V, I   B. II, IV, I, V, III   C. V, III, II, IV, I   D. III, II, IV, I, V

19. I. After the Romans left Britain, there were relentless attacks on the islands from the barbarian tribes of northern Germany—the Angles, Saxons, and Jutes.
II. As the empire weakened, Roman soldiers withdrew from Britain, leaving behind a country that continued to practice the Christian religion that had been introduced by the Romans.
III. Early Latin writings tell of a Christian warrior named Arturius (Arthur, in English) who led the British citizens to defeat these barbarian invades, and brought an extended period of peace to the lands of Britain.
IV. Long ago, the British Isles were part of the far-flung Roman Empire that extended across most of Europe and into Africa and Asia.
V. The romantic legend of King Arthur and his knights of the Round Table, one of the most popular and widespread stories of all time, appears to have some foundation in history.

The BEST order is:
A. V, IV, III, II, I   B. V, IV, II, I, III   C. IV, V, II, III, I   D. IV, III, II, I, V

20. I. The cylinder was allowed to cool until it could stand on its own, and then it was cut from the tube and split down the side with a single straight cut.
II. Nineteenth-century glassmakers, who had not yet discovered the glazier's modern techniques for making panes of glass, had to create a method for converting their blown gas into flat sheets.
III. The bubble was then pierced at the end to make a hole that opened up while the glassmaker gently spun it, creating a cylinder of glass.
IV. Turned on its side and laid on a conveyor belt, the cylinder was strengthened, or tempered, by being heated again and cooled very slowly, eventually flattening out into a single rectangular of glass.
V. To do this, the glassmaker dipped the end of a long tube into melted glass and blew into the other end of the tube, creating an expanding bubble of glass.

The BEST order is:
A. II, V, III, IV, I   B. II, IV, V, III, I   C. III, V, II, IV, I   D. III, I, IV, V, II

21. I. The splints are almost always hidden, but horses are occasionally born whose splinted toes project from the leg on either side, just above the hoof.
II. The second and fourth toes remained, but shrank to thin splints of bone that fused invisibly to the horse's leg bone.
III. Horses are unique among mammals, having evolved feet that each end in what is essentially a single toe, capped by a large, sturdy hoof.
IV. Julius Caesar, an emperor of ancient Rome, was said to have owned one of these three-toed horses, and considered it so special that he would not permit anyone else to ride it.
V. Though the horse's earlier ancestors possessed the traditional mammalian set of five toes on each foot, the horse has retained only its third toe; its first and fifth toes disappeared completely as the horse evolved.
The BEST order is:
A. III, V, II, I, IV   B. V, III, II, IV, I   C. III, II, V, I, IV   D. V, II, III, I, IV

22. I. The new building materials—some of which are twenty feet long, and weigh nearly six tons—were transported to Pohnpei on rafts, and were brought into their present position by using hibiscus fiber ropes and leverage to move the stone columns upward along the inclined trunks of coconut palm trees.
II. The ancestors built great fires to heat the stone, and then poured cool seawater on the columns, which caused the stone to contract and split along natural fracture lines.
III. The now-abandoned enclave of Nan Madol, a group of 92 man-made islands off the shore of the Micronesian island of Pohnpei, is estimated to have been built around the year 500 A.D.
IV. The islanders say their ancestors quarried stone columns from a nearby island, where large basalt columns were formed by the cooling of molten lava.
V. The structures of Nan Madol are remarkable for the sheer size of some of the stone "longs" or columns that were used to create the walls of the offshore community, and today anthropologists can only rely on the information of existing local people for clues about how Nan Madol was built.
The BEST order is:
A. V, IV, III, II, I   B. V, III, I, IV, II   C. III, V, IV, II, I   D. III, I, IV, II, V

23. I. One of the most easily manipulated substances on earth, glass can be made into ceramic tiles that are composed of over 90% air.
II. NASA's space shuttles are the first spacecraft ever designed to leave and re-enter the earth's atmosphere while remaining intact.
III. These ceramic tiles are such effective insulators that when a tile emerges from the oven in which it was fired, it can be held safely in a person's hand by the edges while its interior still glows at a temperature well over 2000°F.
IV. Eventually, the engineers were led to a material that is as old as our most ancient civilization.
V. Because the temperature during atmospheric re-entry is so incredibly hot, it took NASA's engineers some time to find a substance capable of protecting the shuttles.

The BEST order is:
A. V, II, I, II, IV   B. II, V, IV, I, III   C. II, III, I, IV, V   D. V, IV, III, I, II

24. I. The secret to teaching any parakeet to talk is patience, and the understanding that when a bird talks," it is simply imitating what it hears, rather than putting ideas into words.
    II. You should stay just out of sight of the bird and repeat the phrase you want it to learn, for at least fifteen minutes every morning and evening.
    III. It is important to leave the bird without any words of encouragement or farewell; otherwise it might combine stray remarks or phrases, such as "Good night," with the phrase you are trying to teach it.
    IV. For this reason, to train your bird to imitate your words you should keep it free of any distractions, especially other noises, while you are giving it "lesson."
    V. After your repetition, you should quietly leave the bird alone for a while, to think over what it has just heard.
    The BEST order is:
    A. I, IV, II, V, III   B. I, II, IV, III, V   C. III, II, I, V, IV   D. III, I, V, IV, II

25. I. As a school approaches, fishermen from neighboring communities join their fishing boats together as a fleet, and string their gill nets together to make a huge fence that is held up by cork floats.
    II. At a signal from the party leaders, or *nakura*, the family members pound the sides of the boats or beat the water with long poles, creating a sudden and deafening noise.
    III. The fishermen work together to drag the trap into a half-circle that may reach 300 yards in diameter, and then the families move their boats to form the other half of the circle around the school of fish.
    IV. The school of fish flee from the commotion into the awaiting trap, where a final wall of net is thrown over the open end of the half-circle, securing the day's haul.
    V. Indonesian people from the area around the Sulu islands live on the sea, in floating villages made of lashed-together or stilted homes, and make much of their living by fishing their home waters for migrating schools of snapper, scad, and other fish.
    The BEST order is:
    A. I, V, III, IV, II   B. I, II, IV, III, V   C. V, I, II, III, IV   D. V, I, III, II, IV

KEY (CORRECT ANSWERS)

1.	D	11.	C
2.	D	12.	A
3.	B	13.	D
4.	A	14.	C
5.	C	15.	D
6.	C	16.	C
7.	D	17.	A
8.	D	18.	D
9.	A	19.	B
10.	B	20.	A

21. A
22. C
23. B
24. A
25. D

PHILOSOPHY, PRINCIPLES, PRACTICES, AND TECHNICS OF SUPERVISION, ADMINISTRATION, MANAGEMENT, AND ORGANIZATION

TABLE OF CONTENTS

	Page
MEANING OF SUPERVISION	1
THE OLD AND THE NEW SUPERVISION	1
THE EIGHT (8) BASIC PRINCIPLES OF THE NEW SUPERVISION	1
I. Principle of Responsibility	1
II. Principle of Authority	2
III. Principle of Self-Growth	2
IV. Principle of Individual Worth	2
V. Principle of Creative Leadership	2
VI. Principle of Success and Failure	2
VII. Principle of Science	3
VIII. Principle of Cooperation	3
WHAT IS ADMINISTRATION?	3
I. Practices Commonly Classed as "Supervisory"	3
II. Practices Commonly Classed as "Administrative"	3
III. Practices Commonly Classed as Both "Supervisory" and "Administrative"	4
RESPONSIBILITIES OF THE SUPERVISOR	4
COMPETENCIES OF THE SUPERVISOR	4
THE PROFESSIONAL SUPERVISOR-EMPLOYEE RELATIONSHIP	4
MINI-TEXT IN SUPERVISION, ADMINISTRATION, MANAGEMENT, AND ORGANIZATION	5
I. Brief Highlights	5
A. Levels of Management	6
B. What the Supervisor Must Learn	6
C. A Definition of Supervision	6
D. Elements of the Team Concept	6
E. Principles of Organization	6
F. The Four Important Parts of Every Job	7
G. Principles of Delegation	7
H. Principles of Effective Communications	7
I. Principles of Work Improvement	7
J. Areas of Job Improvement	7
K. Seven Key Points in Making Improvements	8

	L.	Corrective Techniques for Job Improvement	8
	M.	A Planning Checklist	8
	N.	Five Characteristics of Good Directions	9
	O.	Types of Directions	9
	P.	Controls	9
	Q.	Orienting the New Employee	9
	R.	Checklist for Orienting New Employees	9
	S.	Principles of Learning	10
	T.	Causes of Poor Performance	10
	U.	Four Major Steps in On-the-Job Instructions	10
	V.	Employees Want Five Things	10
	W.	Some Don'ts in Regard to Praise	11
	X.	How to Gain Your Workers' Confidence	11
	Y.	Sources of Employee Problems	11
	Z.	The Supervisor's Key to Discipline	11
	AA.	Five Important Processes of Management	12
	BB.	When the Supervisor Fails to Plan	12
	CC.	Fourteen General Principles of Management	12
	DD.	Change	12
II.	Brief Topical Summaries		13
	A.	Who/What is the Supervisor?	13
	B.	The Sociology of Work	13
	C.	Principles and Practices of Supervision	14
	D.	Dynamic Leadership	14
	E.	Processes for Solving Problems	15
	F.	Training for Results	15
	G.	Health, Safety, and Accident Prevention	16
	H.	Equal Employment Opportunity	16
	I.	Improving Communications	16
	J.	Self-Development	17
	K.	Teaching and Training	17
		1. The Teaching Process	17
		a. Preparation	17
		b. Presentation	18
		c. Summary	18
		d. Application	18
		e. Evaluation	18
		2. Teaching Methods	18
		a. Lecture	18
		b. Discussion	18
		c. Demonstration	19
		d. Performance	19
		e. Which Method to Use	19

PHILOSOPHY, PRINCIPLES, PRACTICES, AND TECHNICS
OF
SUPERVISION, ADMINISTRATION, MANAGEMENT, AND ORGANIZATION

MEANING OF SUPERVISION

The extension of the democratic philosophy has been accompanied by an extension in the scope of supervision. Modern leaders and supervisors no longer think of supervision in the narrow sense of being confined chiefly to visiting employees, supplying materials, or rating the staff. They regard supervision as being intimately related to all the concerned agencies of society, they speak of the supervisor's function in terms of "growth," rather than the "improvement" of employees.

This modern concept of supervision may be defined as follows: Supervision is leadership and the development of leadership within groups which are cooperatively engaged in inspection, research, training, guidance, and evaluation.

THE OLD AND THE NEW SUPERVISION

TRADITIONAL
1. Inspection
2. Focused on the employee
3. Visitation
4. Random and haphazard
5. Imposed and authoritarian
6. One person usually

MODERN
1. Study and analysis
2. Focused on aims, materials, methods, supervisors, employees, environment
3. Demonstrations, intervisitation, workshops, directed reading, bulletins, etc.
4. Definitely organized and planned (scientific)
5. Cooperative and democratic
6. Many persons involved (creative)

THE EIGHT (8) BASIC PRINCIPLES OF THE NEW SUPERVISION

I. Principle of Responsibility
   Authority to act and responsibility for acting must be joined.
   A. If you give responsibility, give authority.
   B. Define employee duties clearly.
   C. Protect employees from criticism by others.
   D. Recognize the rights as well as obligations of employees.
   E. Achieve the aims of a democratic society insofar as it is possible within the area of your work.
   F. Establish a situation favorable to training and learning.
   G. Accept ultimate responsibility for everything done in your section, unit, office, division, department.
   H. Good administration and good supervision are inseparable.

II. Principle of Authority
The success of the supervisor is measured by the extent to which the power of authority is not used.
   A. Exercise simplicity and informality in supervision
   B. Use the simplest machinery of supervision
   C. If it is good for the organization as a whole, it is probably justified.
   D. Seldom be arbitrary or authoritative.
   E. Do not base your work on the power of position or of personality.
   F. Permit and encourage the free expression of opinions.

III. Principle of Self-Growth
The success of the supervisor is measured by the extent to which, and the speed with which, he is no longer needed.
   A. Base criticism on principles, not on specifics.
   B. Point out higher activities to employees.
   C. Train for self-thinking by employees to meet new situations.
   D. Stimulate initiative, self-reliance, and individual responsibility
   E. Concentrate on stimulating the growth of employees rather than on removing defects.

IV. Principle of Individual Worth
Respect for the individual is a paramount consideration in supervision.
   A. Be human and sympathetic in dealing with employees.
   B. Don't nag about things to be done.
   C. Recognize the individual differences among employees and seek opportunities to permit best expression of each personality.

V. Principle of Creative Leadership
The best supervision is that which is not apparent to the employee.
   A. Stimulate, don't drive employees to creative action.
   B. Emphasize doing good things.
   C. Encourage employees to do what they do best.
   D. Do not be too greatly concerned with details of subject or method.
   E. Do not be concerned exclusively with immediate problems and activities.
   F. Reveal higher activities and make them both desired and maximally possible.
   G. Determine procedures in the light of each situation but see that these are derived from a sound basic philosophy.
   H. Aid, inspire, and lead so as to liberate the creative spirit latent in all good employees.

VI. Principle of Success and Failure
There are no unsuccessful employees, only unsuccessful supervisors who have failed to give proper leadership.
   A. Adapt suggestions to the capacities, attitudes, and prejudices of employees.
   B. Be gradual, be progressive, be persistent.
   C. Help the employee find the general principle; have the employee apply his own problem to the general principle.
   D. Give adequate appreciation for good work and honest effort.
   E. Anticipate employee difficulties and help to prevent them.
   F. Encourage employees to do the desirable things they will do anyway.
   G. Judge your supervision by the results it secures.

VII. Principle of Science
Successful supervision is scientific, objective, and experimental. It is based on facts, not on prejudices.
   A. Be cumulative in results.
   B. Never divorce your suggestions from the goals of training.
   C. Don't be impatient of results.
   D. Keep all matters on a professional, not a personal, level.
   E. Do not be concerned exclusively with immediate problems and activities.
   F. Use objective means of determining achievement and rating where possible.

VIII. Principle of Cooperation
Supervision is a cooperative enterprise between supervisor and employee.
   A. Begin with conditions as they are.
   B. Ask opinions of all involved when formulating policies.
   C. Organization is as good as its weakest link.
   D. Let employees help to determine policies and department programs.
   E. Be approachable and accessible—physically and mentally.
   F. Develop pleasant social relationships.

WHAT IS ADMINISTRATION

Administration is concerned with providing the environment, the material facilities, and the operational procedures that will promote the maximum growth and development of supervisors and employees. (Organization is an aspect and a concomitant of administration.)

There is no sharp line of demarcation between supervision and administration; these functions are intimately interrelated and, often, overlapping. They are complementary activities.

I. Practices Commonly Classed as "Supervisory"
   A. Conducting employees' conferences
   B. Visiting sections, units, offices, divisions, departments
   C. Arranging for demonstrations
   D. Examining plans
   E. Suggesting professional reading
   F. Interpreting bulletins
   G. Recommending in-service training courses
   H. Encouraging experimentation
   I. Appraising employee morale
   J. Providing for intervisitation

II. Practices Commonly Classified as "Administrative"
   A. Management of the office
   B. Arrangement of schedules for extra duties
   C. Assignment of rooms or areas
   D. Distribution of supplies
   E. Keeping records and reports
   F. Care of audio-visual materials
   G. Keeping inventory records
   H. Checking record cards and books

I. Programming special activities
J. Checking on the attendance and punctuality of employees

III. Practices Commonly Classified as Both "Supervisory" and "Administrative"
A. Program construction
B. Testing or evaluating outcomes
C. Personnel accounting
D. Ordering instructional materials

RESPONSIBILITIES OF THE SUPERVISOR

A person employed in a supervisory capacity must constantly be able to improve his own efficiency and ability. He represent the employer to the employees and only continuous self-examination can make him a capable supervisor.

Leadership and training are the supervisor's responsibility. An efficient working unit is one in which the employees work with the supervisor. It is his job to bring out the best in his employees. He must always be relaxed, courteous, and calm in his association with his employees. Their feelings are important, and a harsh attitude does not develop the most efficient employees.

COMPETENCES OF THE SUPERVISOR

I. Complete knowledge of the duties and responsibilities of his position.
II. To be able to organize a job, plan ahead, and carry through.
III. To have self-confidence and initiative.
IV. To be able to handle the unexpected situation and make quick decisions.
V. To be able to properly train subordinates in the positions they are best suited for.
VI. To be able to keep good human relations among his subordinates.
VII. To be able to keep good human relations between his subordinates and himself and to earn their respect and trust.

THE PROFESSIONAL SUPERVISOR-EMPLOYEE RELATIONSHIP

There are two kinds of efficiency: one kind is only apparent and is produced in organizations through the exercise of mere discipline; this is but a simulation of the second, or true, efficiency which springs from spontaneous cooperation. If you are a manager, no matter how great or small your responsibility, it is your job, in the final analysis, to create and develop this involuntary cooperation among the people whom you supervise. For, no matter how powerful a combination of money, machines, and materials a company may have, this is a dead and sterile thing without a team of willing, thinking, and articulate people to guide it.

The following 21 points are presented as indicative of the exemplary basic relationship that should exist between supervisor and employee:

1. Each person wants to be liked and respected by his fellow employee and wants to be treated with consideration and respect by his superior.
2. The most competent employee will make an error. However, in a unit where good relations exist between the supervisor and his employees, tenseness and fear do not exist. Thus, errors are not hidden or covered up, and the efficiency of a unit is not impaired.

3. Subordinates resent rules, regulations, or orders that are unreasonable or unexplained.
4. Subordinates are quick to resent unfairness, harshness, injustices, and favoritism.
5. An employee will accept responsibility if he knows that he will be complimented for a job well done, and not too harshly chastised for failure; that his supervisor will check the cause of the failure, and, if it was the supervisor's fault, he will assume the blame therefore. If it was the employee's fault, his supervisor will explain the correct method or means of handling the responsibility.
6. An employee wants to receive credit for a suggestion he has made, that is used. If a suggestion cannot be used, the employee is entitled to an explanation. The supervisor should not say "no" and close the subject.
7. Fear and worry slow up a worker's ability. Poor working environment can impair his physical and mental health. A good supervisor avoids forceful methods, threats, and arguments to get a job done.
8. A forceful supervisor is able to train his employees individually and as a team, and is able to motivate them in the proper channels.
9. A mature supervisor is able to properly evaluate his subordinates and to keep them happy and satisfied.
10. A sensitive supervisor will never patronize his subordinates.
11. A worthy supervisor will respect his employees' confidences.
12. Definite and clear-cut responsibilities should be assigned to each executive.
13. Responsibility should always be coupled with corresponding authority.
14. No change should be made in the scope or responsibilities of a position without a definite understanding to that effect on the part of all persons concerned.
15. No executive or employee, occupying a single position in the organization, should be subject to definite orders from more than one source.
16. Orders should never be given to subordinates over the head of a responsible executive. Rather than do this, the officer in question should be supplanted.
17. Criticisms of subordinates should, whoever possible, be made privately, and in no case should a subordinate be criticized in the presence of executives or employees of equal or lower rank.
18. No dispute or difference between executives or employees as to authority or responsibilities should be considered too trivial for prompt and careful adjudication.
19. Promotions, wage changes, and disciplinary action should always be approved by the executive immediately superior to the one directly responsible.
20. No executive or employee should ever be required, or expected, to be at the same time an assistant to, and critic of, another.
21. Any executive whose work is subject to regular inspection should, wherever practicable, be given the assistance and facilities necessary to enable him to maintain an independent check of the quality of his work.

MINI-TEXT IN SUPERVISION, ADMINISTRATION, MANAGEMENT, AND ORGANIZATION

I. Brief Highlights

Listed concisely and sequentially are major headings and important data in the field for quick recall and review.

A. Levels of Management
Any organization of some size has several levels of management. In terms of a ladder, the levels are:

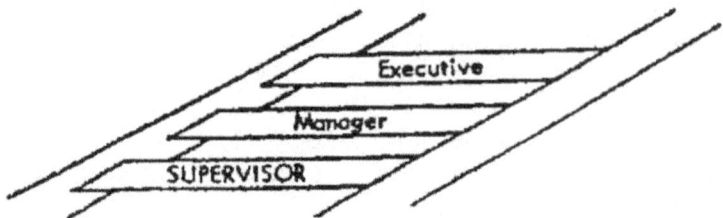

The first level is very important because it is the beginning point of management leadership.

B. What the Supervisor Must Learn
A supervisor must learn to:
1. Deal with people and their differences
2. Get the job done through people
3. Recognize the problems when they exist
4. Overcome obstacles to good performance
5. Evaluate the performance of people
6. Check his own performance in terms of accomplishment

C. A Definition of Supervisor
The term supervisor means any individual having authority, in the interests of the employer, to hire, transfer, suspend, lay-off, recall, promote, discharge, assign, reward, or discipline other employees or responsibility to direct them, or to adjust their grievances, or effectively to recommend such action, if, in connection with the foregoing, exercise of such authority is not of a merely routine or clerical nature but requires the use of independent judgment.

D. Elements of the Team Concept
What is involved in teamwork? The component parts are:
1. Members
2. A leader
3. Goals
4. Plans
5. Cooperation
6. Spirit

E. Principles of Organization
1. A team member must know what his job is.
2. Be sure that the nature and scope of a job are understood.
3. Authority and responsibility should be carefully spelled out.
4. A supervisor should be permitted to make the maximum number of decisions affecting his employees.
5. Employees should report to only one supervisor.
6. A supervisor should direct only as many employees as he can handle effectively.
7. An organization plan should be flexible.

8. Inspection and performance of work should be separate.
9. Organizational problems should receive immediate attention.
10. Assign work in line with ability and experience.

F. The Four Important Parts of Every Job
1. Inherent in every job is the *accountability* for results.
2. A second set of factors in every job is *responsibilities*.
3. Along with duties and responsibilities one must have the *authority* to act within certain limits without obtaining permission to proceed.
4. No job exists in a vacuum. The supervisor is surrounded by key *relationships*.

G. Principles of Delegation
Where work is delegated for the first time, the supervisor should think in terms of these questions:
1. Who is best qualified to do this?
2. Can an employee improve his abilities by doing this?
3. How long should an employee spend on this?
4. Are there any special problems for which he will need guidance?
5. How broad a delegation can I make?

H. Principles of Effective Communications
1. Determine the media.
2. To whom directed?
3. Identification and source authority.
4. Is communication understood?

I. Principles of Work Improvement
1. Most people usually do only the work which is assigned to them.
2. Workers are likely to fit assigned work into the time available to perform it.
3. A good workload usually stimulates output.
4. People usually do their best work when they know that results will be reviewed or inspected.
5. Employees usually feel that someone else is responsible for conditions of work, workplace layout, job methods, type of tools/equipment, and other such factors.
6. Employees are usually defensive about their job security.
7. Employees have natural resistance to change.
8. Employees can support or destroy a supervisor.
9. A supervisor usually earns the respect of his people through his personal example of diligence and efficiency.

J. Areas of Job Improvement
The areas of job improvement are quite numerous, but the most common ones which a supervisor can identify and utilize are:
1. Departmental layout
2. Flow of work
3. Workplace layout
4. Utilization of manpower
5. Work methods
6. Materials handling

7. Utilization
8. Motion economy

K. Seven Key Points in Making Improvements
1. Select the job to be improved
2. Study how it is being done now
3. Question the present method
4. Determine actions to be taken
5. Chart proposed method
6. Get approval and apply
7. Solicit worker participation

l. Corrective Techniques of Job Improvement
Specific Problems
1. Size of workload
2. Inability to meet schedules
3. Strain and fatigue
4. Improper use of men and skills
5. Waste, poor quality, unsafe conditions
6. Bottleneck conditions that hinder output
7. Poor utilization of equipment and machine
8. Efficiency and productivity of labor

General Improvement
1. Departmental layout
2. Flow of work
3. Work plan layout
4. Utilization of manpower
5. Work methods
6. Materials handling
7. Utilization of equipment
8. Motion economy

Corrective Techniques
1. Study with scale model
2. Flow chart study
3. Motion analysis
4. Comparison of units produced to standard allowance
5. Methods analysis
6. Flow chart and equipment study
7. Down time vs. running time
8. Motion analysis

M. A Planning Checklist
1. Objectives
2. Controls
3. Delegations
4. Communications
5. Resources
6. Manpower

7. Equipment
8. Supplies and materials
9. Utilization of time
10. Safety
11. Money
12. Work
13. Timing of improvements

N. Five Characteristics of Good Directions
In order to get results, directions must be:
1. Possible of accomplishment
2. Agreeable with worker interests
3. Related to mission
4. Planned and complete
5. Unmistakably clear

O. Types of Directions
1. Demands or direct orders
2. Requests
3. Suggestion or implication
4. volunteering

P. Controls
A typical listing of the overall areas in which the supervisor should establish controls might be:
1. Manpower
2. Materials
3. Quality of work
4. Quantity of work
5. Time
6. Space
7. Money
8. Methods

Q. Orienting the New Employee
1. Prepare for him
2. Welcome the new employee
3. Orientation for the job
4. Follow-up

R. Checklist for Orienting New Employees   Yes   No
1. Do you appreciate the feelings of new employees
   when they first report for work?   ___   ___
2. Are you aware of the fact that the new employee must
   make a big adjustment to his job?   ___   ___
3. Have you given him good reasons for liking the job and
   the organization?   ___   ___
4. Have you prepared for his first day on the job?   ___   ___
5. Did you welcome him cordially and make him feel needed?   ___   ___

                                                                              Yes   No

    6. Did you establish rapport with him so that he feels free to talk and discuss matters with you?

    7. Did you explain his job to him and his relationship to you?

    8. Does he know that his work will be evaluated periodically on a basis that is fair and objective?

    9. Did you introduce him to his fellow workers in such a way that they are likely to accept him?

    10. Does he know what employee benefits he will receive?

    11. Does he understand the importance of being on the job and what to do if he must leave his duty station?

    12. Has he been impressed with the importance of accident prevention and safe practice?

    13. Does he generally know his way around the department?

    14. Is he under the guidance of a sponsor who will teach the right way of doing things?

    15. Do you plan to follow-up so that he will continue to adjust successfully to his job?

S. Principles of Learning
1. Motivation
2. Demonstration or explanation
3. Practice

T. Causes of Poor Performance
1. Improper training for job
2. Wrong tools
3. Inadequate directions
4. Lack of supervisory follow-up
5. Poor communications
6. Lack of standards of performance
7. Wrong work habits
8. Low morale
9. Other

U. Four Major Steps in On-The-Job Instruction
1. Prepare the worker
2. Present the operation
3. Tryout performance
4. Follow-up

V. Employees Want Five Things
1. Security
2. Opportunity
3. Recognition
4. Inclusion
5. Expression

W. Some Don'ts in Regard to Praise
1. Don't praise a person for something he hasn't done.
2. Don't praise a person unless you can be sincere.
3. Don't be sparing in praise just because your superior withholds it from you.
4. Don't let too much time elapse between good performance and recognition of it

X. How to Gain Your Workers' Confidence
Methods of developing confidence include such things as:
1. Knowing the interests, habits, hobbies of employees
2. Admitting your own inadequacies
3. Sharing and telling of confidence in others
4. Supporting people when they are in trouble
5. Delegating matters that can be well handled
6. Being frank and straightforward about problems and working conditions
7. Encouraging others to bring their problems to you
8. Taking action on problems which impede worker progress

Y. Sources of Employee Problems
On-the-job causes might be such things as:
1. A feeling that favoritism is exercised in assignments
2. Assignment of overtime
3. An undue amount of supervision
4. Changing methods or systems
5. Stealing of ideas or trade secrets
6. Lack of interest in job
7. Threat of reduction in force
8. Ignorance or lack of communications
9. Poor equipment
10. Lack of knowing how supervisor feels toward employee
11. Shift assignments

Off-the-job problems might have to do with:
1. Health
2. Finances
3. Housing
4. Family

Z. The Supervisor's Key to Discipline
There are several key points about discipline which the supervisor should keep in mind:
1. Job discipline is one of the disciplines of life and is directed by the supervisor.
2. It is more important to correct an employee fault than to fix blame for it.
3. Employee performance is affected by problems both on the job and off.
4. Sudden or abrupt changes in behavior can be indications of important employee problems.
5. Problems should be dealt with as soon as possible after they are identified.
6. The attitude of the supervisor may have more to do with solving problems than the techniques of problem solving.
7. Correction of employee behavior should be resorted to only after the supervisor is sure that training or counseling will not be helpful.

8. Be sure to document your disciplinary actions.
9. Make sure that you are disciplining on the basis of facts rather than personal feelings.
10. Take each disciplinary step in order, being careful not to make snap judgments, or decisions based on impatience.

AA. Five Important Processes of Management
1. Planning
2. Organizing
3. Scheduling
4. Controlling
5. Motivating

BB. When the Supervisor Fails to Plan
1. Supervisor creates impression of not knowing his job
2. May lead to excessive overtime
3. Job runs itself—supervisor lacks control
4. Deadlines and appointments missed
5. Parts of the work go undone
6. Work interrupted by emergencies
7. Sets a bad example
8. Uneven workload creates peaks and valleys
9. Too much time on minor details at expense of more important tasks

CC. Fourteen General Principles of Management
1. Division of work
2. Authority and responsibility
3. Discipline
4. Unity of command
5. Unity of direction
6. Subordination of individual interest to general interest
7. Remuneration of personnel
8. Centralization
9. Scalar chain
10. Order
11. Equity
12. Stability of tenure of personnel
13. Initiative
14. Esprit de corps

DD. Change

Bringing about change is perhaps attempted more often, and yet less well understood, than anything else the supervisor does. How do people generally react to change? (People tend to resist change that is imposed upon them by other individuals or circumstances.

Change is characteristic of every situation. It is a part of every real endeavor where the efforts of people are concerned.

1. Why do people resist change?
   People may resist change because of:
   a. Fear of the unknown
   b. Implied criticism
   c. Unpleasant experiences in the past
   d. Fear of loss of status
   e. Threat to the ego
   f. Fear of loss of economic stability

2. How can we best overcome the resistance to change?
   In initiating change, take these steps:
   a. Get ready to sell
   b. Identify sources of help
   c. Anticipate objections
   d. Sell benefits
   e. Listen in depth
   f. Follow up

II. Brief Topical Summaries

   A. Who/What is the Supervisor?
      1. The supervisor is often called the "highest level employee and the lowest level manager."
      2. A supervisor is a member of both management and the work group. He acts as a bridge between the two.
      3. Most problems in supervision are in the area of human relations, or people problems.
      4. Employees expect: Respect, opportunity to learn and to advance, and a sense of belonging, and so forth.
      5. Supervisors are responsible for directing people and organizing work. Planning is of paramount importance.
      6. A position description is a set of duties and responsibilities inherent to a given position.
      7. It is important to keep the position description up-to-date and to provide each employee with his own copy.

   B. The Sociology of Work
      1. People are alike in many ways; however, each individual is unique.
      2. The supervisor is challenged in getting to know employee differences. Acquiring skills in evaluating individuals is an asset.
      3. Maintaining meaningful working relationships in the organization is of great importance.
      4. The supervisor has an obligation to help individuals to develop to their fullest potential.
      5. Job rotation on a planned basis helps to build versatility and to maintain interest and enthusiasm in work groups.
      6. Cross training (job rotation) provides backup skills.

7. The supervisor can help reduce tension by maintaining a sense of humor, providing guidance to employees, and by making reasonable and timely decisions. Employees respond favorably to working under reasonably predictable circumstances.
8. Change is characteristic of all managerial behavior. The supervisor must adjust to changes in procedures, new methods, technological changes, and to a number of new and sometimes challenging situations.
9. To overcome the natural tendency for people to resist change, the supervisor should become more skillful in initiating change.

C. Principles and Practices of Supervision
1. Employees should be required to answer to only one superior.
2. A supervisor can effectively direct only a limited number of employees, depending upon the complexity, variety, and proximity of the jobs involved.
3. The organizational chart presents the organization in graphic form. It reflects lines of authority and responsibility as well as interrelationships of units within the organization.
4. Distribution of work can be improved through an analysis using the "Work Distribution Chart."
5. The "Work Distribution Chart" reflects the division of work within a unit in understandable form.
6. When related tasks are given to an employee, he has a better chance of increasing his skills through training.
7. The individual who is given the responsibility for tasks must also be given the appropriate authority to insure adequate results.
8. The supervisor should delegate repetitive, routine work. Preparation of recurring reports, maintaining leave and attendance records are some examples.
9. Good discipline is essential to good task performance. Discipline is reflected in the actions of employees on the job in the absence of supervision.
10. Disciplinary action may have to be taken when the positive aspects of discipline have failed. Reprimand, warning, and suspension are examples of disciplinary action.
11. If a situation calls for a reprimand, be sure it is deserved and remember it is to be done in private.

D. Dynamic Leadership
1. A style is a personal method or manner of exerting influence.
2. Authoritarian leaders often see themselves as the source of power and authority.
3. The democratic leader often perceives the group as the source of authority and power.
4. Supervisors tend to do better when using the pattern of leadership that is most natural for them.
5. Social scientists suggest that the effective supervisor use the leadership style that best fits the problem or circumstances involved.
6. All four styles—telling, selling, consulting, joining—have their place. Using one does not preclude using the other at another time.

7. The theory X point of view assumes that the average person dislikes work, will avoid it whenever possible, and must be coerced to achieve organizational objectives.
8. The theory Y point of view assumes that the average person considers work to be a natural as play, and, when the individual is committed, he requires little supervision or direction to accomplish desired objectives.
9. The leader's basic assumptions concerning human behavior and human nature affect his actions, decisions, and other managerial practices.
10. Dissatisfaction among employees is often present, but difficult to isolate. The supervisor should seek to weaken dissatisfaction by keeping promises, being sincere and considerate, keeping employees informed, and so forth.
11. Constructive suggestions should be encouraged during the natural progress of the work.

E. Processes for Solving Problems
1. People find their daily tasks more meaningful and satisfying when they can improve them.
2. The causes of problems, or the key factors, are often hidden in the background. Ability to solve problems often involves the ability to isolate them from their backgrounds. There is some substance to the cliché that some persons "can't see the forest for the trees."
3. New procedures are often developed from old ones. Problems should be broken down into manageable parts. New ideas can be adapted from old one.
4. People think differently in problem-solving situations. Using a logical, patterned approach is often useful. One approach found to be useful includes these steps:
   a. Define the problem
   b. Establish objectives
   c. Get the facts
   d. Weigh and decide
   e. Take action
   f. Evaluate action

F. Training for Results
1. Participants respond best when they feel training is important to them.
2. The supervisor has responsibility for the training and development of those who report to him.
3. When training is delegated to others, great care must be exercised to insure the trainer has knowledge, aptitude, and interest for his work as a trainer.
4. Training (learning) of some type goes on continually. The most successful supervisor makes certain the learning contributes in a productive manner to operational goals.
5. New employees are particularly susceptible to training. Older employees facing new job situations require specific training, as well as having need for development and growth opportunities.
6. Training needs require continuous monitoring.
7. The training officer of an agency is a professional with a responsibility to assist supervisors in solving training problems.

8. Many of the self-development steps important to the supervisor's own growth are equally important to the development of peers and subordinates. Knowledge of these is important when the supervisor consults with others on development and growth opportunities.

G. Health, Safety, and Accident Prevention
1. Management-minded supervisors take appropriate measures to assist employees in maintaining health and in assuring safe practices in the work environment.
2. Effective safety training and practices help to avoid injury and accidents.
3. Safety should be a management goal. All infractions of safety which are observed should be corrected without exception.
4. Employees' safety attitude, training and instruction, provision of safe tools and equipment, supervision, and leadership are considered highly important factors which contribute to safety and which can be influenced directly by supervisors.
5. When accidents do occur, they should be investigated promptly for very important reasons, including the fact that information which is gained can be used to prevent accidents in the future.

H. Equal Employment Opportunity
1. The supervisor should endeavor to treat all employees fairly, without regard to religion, race, sex, or national origin.
2. Groups tend to reflect the attitude of the leader. Prejudice can be detected even in very subtle form. Supervisors must strive to create a feeling of mutual respect and confidence in every employee.
3. Complete utilization of all human resources is a national goal. Equitable consideration should be accorded women in the work force, minority-group members, the physically and mentally handicapped, and the older employee. The important question is: "Who can do the job?"
4. Training opportunities, recognition for performance, overtime assignments, promotional opportunities, and all other personnel actions are to be handled on an equitable basis.

I. Improving Communications
1. Communications is achieving understanding between the sender and the receiver of a message. It also means sharing information—the creation of understanding.
2. Communication is basic to all human activity. Words are means of conveying meanings; however, real meanings are in people.
3. There are very practical differences in the effectiveness of one-way, impersonal, and two-way communications. Words spoken face-to-face are better understood. Telephone conversations are effective, but lack the rapport of person-to-person exchanges. The whole person communicates.
4. Cooperation and communication in an organization go hand in hand. When there is a mutual respect between people, spelling out rules and procedures for communicating is unnecessary.
5. There are several barriers to effective communications. These include failure to listen with respect and understanding, lack of skill in feedback, and misinterpreting the meanings of words used by the speaker. It is also common

practice to listen to what we want to hear, and tune out things we do not want to hear.
6. Communication is management's chief problem. The supervisor should accept the challenge to communicate more effectively and to improve interagency and intra-agency communications.
7. The supervisor may often plan for and conduct meetings. The planning phase is critical and may determine the success or the failure of a meeting.
8. Speaking before groups usually requires extra effort. Stage fright may never disappear completely, but it can be controlled.

J. Self-Development
1. Every employee is responsible for his own self-development.
2. Toastmaster and toastmistress clubs offer opportunities to improve skills in oral communications.
3. Planning for one's own self-development is of vital importance. Supervisors know their own strengths and limitations better than anyone else.
4. Many opportunities are open to aid the supervisor in his developmental efforts, including job assignments; training opportunities, both governmental and non-governmental—to include universities and professional conferences and seminars.
5. Programmed instruction offers a means of studying at one's own rate.
6. Where difficulties may arise from a supervisor's being away from his work for training, he may participate in televised home study or correspondence courses to meet his self-development needs.

K. Teaching and Training
1. The Teaching Process
Teaching is encouraging and guiding the learning activities of students toward established goals. In most cases this process consists of five steps: preparation, presentation, summarization, evaluation, and application.

   a. Preparation
   Preparation is two-fold in nature; that of the supervisor and the employee. Preparation by the supervisor is absolutely essential to success. He must know what, when, where, how, and whom he will teach. Some of the factors that should be considered are:
   1) The objectives
   2) The materials needed
   3) The methods to be used
   4) Employee participation
   5) Employee interest
   6) Training aids
   7) Evaluation
   8) Summarization

   Employee preparation consists in preparing the employee to receive the material. Probably the most important single factor in the preparation of the employee is arousing and maintaining his interest. He must know the objectives of the training, why he is there, how the material can be used, and its importance to him.

b. Presentation
In presentation, have a carefully designed plan and follow it. The plan should be accurate and complete, yet flexible enough to meet situations as they arise. The method of presentation will be determined by the particular situation and objectives.

c. Summary
A summary should be made at the end of every training unit and program. In addition, there may be internal summaries depending on the nature of the material being taught. The important thing is that the trainee must always be able to understand how each part of the new material relates to the whole.

d. Application
The supervisor must arrange work so the employee will be given a chance to apply new knowledge or skills while the material is still clear in his mind and interest is high. The trainee does not really know whether he has learned the material until he has been given a chance to apply it. If the material is not applied, it loses most of its value.

e. Evaluation
The purpose of all training is to promote learning. To determine whether the training has been a success or failure, the supervisor must evaluate this learning.
In the broadest sense, evaluation includes all the devices, methods, skills, and techniques used by the supervisor to keep himself and the employees informed as to their progress toward the objectives they are pursuing. The extent to which the employee has mastered the knowledge, skills, and abilities, or changed his attitudes, as determined by the program objectives, is the extent to which instruction has succeeded or failed.
Evaluation should not be confined to the end of the lesson, day, or program but should be used continuously. We shall note later the way this relates to the rest of the teaching process.

2. Teaching Methods
A teaching method is a pattern of identifiable student and instructor activity used in presenting training material.
All supervisors are faced with the problem of deciding which method should be used at a given time.

a. Lecture
The lecture is direct oral presentation of material by the supervisor. The present trend is to place less emphasis on the trainer's activity and more on that of the trainee.

b. Discussion
Teaching by discussion or conference involves using questions and other techniques to arouse interest and focus attention upon certain areas, and by doing so creating a learning situation. This can be one of the most

valuable methods because it gives the employees an opportunity to express their ideas and pool their knowledge.

    c. Demonstration
The demonstration is used to teach how something works or how to do something. It can be used to show a principle or what the results of a series of actions will be. A well-staged demonstration is particularly effective because it shows proper methods of performance in a realistic manner.

    d. Performance
Performance is one of the most fundamental of all learning techniques or teaching methods. The trainee may be able to tell how a specific operation should be performed but he cannot be sure he knows how to perform the operation until he has done so.
As with all methods, there are certain advantages and disadvantages to each method.

    e. Which Method to Use
Moreover, there are other methods and techniques of teaching. It is difficult to use any method without other methods entering into it. In any learning situation, a combination of methods is usually more effective than any one method alone.

Finally, evaluation must be integrated into the other aspects of the teaching-learning process.

It must be used in the motivation of the trainees; it must be used to assist in developing understanding during the training; and it must be related to employee application of the results of training.

This is distinctly the role of the supervisor.

www.ingramcontent.com/pod-product-compliance
Lightning Source LLC
Chambersburg PA
CBHW082205300426
44117CB00016B/2677